The Future
Alien Contact

MICHAEL

The Future Alien Contact
By Mike Brumfield

ISBN # 0-9740390-2-0
Library of Congress Catalog Card Number (Applied For)

Retail $13.50 plus $3.50 shipping.
Expect delivery in two to three weeks.
To order call 931/657-5815.

First Edition, June 2004

Dedication

I would like to dedicate this to the seekers in life. I wake up every day at odds with the world that I live in. What! We aren't spread throughout the universe? No, this can't be real. Mankind is so primitive! The most famous man Yeshua, once gave us a simple command. "Seek, first the kingdom of heaven." I am not a follower, I am a seeker. I am seeking! Primitive man always looked up to the stars of heaven, therefore it must be space. We even named our planets after Greek Gods which live in heaven. Knowledge is power and he called himself the word. As a scientist, I know the power of information and can see obvious cures for the future of mankind. These are made possible with the knowledge of DNA and genetics. We could perfect our babies before they are born and establish one race of mankind, that all look the same.

We could also eliminate sex. The propagation of our species could be better achieved through science. Last but not least, we could abolish religion, as we have the law to make us be good. Religion causes war, sex causes death, and our outward differences perpetuate division. These are the basic plagues of our species.Oh, by the way, we should cap wealth as well. I don't think anybody should be allowed to have more than a million dollars and say they're spiritual. We can scientifically create perfection, but do we really want it? And what if it could only exist by being universally "ugly"? Well, if you find yourself answering no, because it would be boring, then I wish you luck. Mankind is the most brutal being in the infinite universe. If you find yourself wanting peace, then look to the skies and open your eyes for you too can reap "my" million-dollar PRIZE. Read on! According to Yeshua heaven is EVERYWHERE (omni-present), perfect, and its inhabitants are equal. "Heaven is their throne and earth their footstool!" This describes the ancient and modern alien evidence! They've conquered space. Why they stay away is the focus of this book. If you "believe" they're spirits and close your mind to the following pictures, then you are the blind following the blind. You will be a follower of religion and I can't cure you. You have fallen prey to their First Commandment "Thou shalt have no other gods before me." Duh!

This is a brainwashing technique. All other cultures have God and Yeshua says "we are gods"! Religion creates a disease called self-righteousness. Please watch the movie *Frailty*. You must cure yourself. This book is not about right or wrong, truth or lies. It is about the evidence. I will leave you with one more command by Yeshua. It supports my theory about us, "Love others as you love yourself". We love oursleves more than anything else. We are a flawed scientific creation, which has no cure, only a dream. Dreams can come true! I want to live my dream, I want to fly. Flying is the ultimate freedom, "from mankind!"

Love and forgiveness always, Michael.

P.S. Yeshua's name has been falsely changed to Jesus. Religion's heaven is findable, scientifically of course. This is all about "believing" the evidence. Last but not least, if you don't seek, just follow the evidence.

T_{HE} E_{VIDENCE}

Paul Villa photo of flying saucer circa 1960.

Picture on front cover of book 1980.

This is the most important evidence because it shows us, what their gods looked like (aliens), what they came and live in (flying saucers) and why they needed gold (space life and exploration). Hence we have the Biblical quote "Heaven's streets are paved with gold." It is a universal religious theme. Heaven is space, up to primitive man.

Cave drawing of aboriginal god Wandjina. Notice similarity to owl man. Also see halo around above head. This supports 10th planet story of gold replacing ozone and "who" was mining it before they created man as a "tiller of the ground" in Genesis. Man's purpose supports skeletal discoveries in gold mines.

The Five Faces of Man

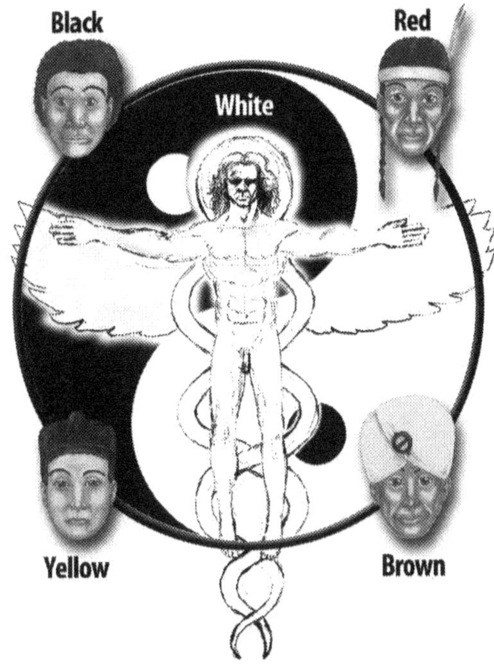

The different colors and facial structures indicate the competition to make the "prettiest" human. This "prettiest" factor is evident in Genesis 6:4 and the fall of the angel story!

Looks give us power over one another. All religions have a fall from heaven and earth being one, void and without form, to being separated. The gods/angels live in space—Earth's become prison. This resulted from a power struggle. The biblical account gives us two creations. Nature created primitive man and then the gods/angels scientifically created modern man as a worker. Modern man is the mystery. The evidence universally points to mining gold. This started 100,000 years ago and continues to this day! The matching yin and yang and AMA symbol to the science symbols of the sperm/egg and DNA reflects our scientific creation. Even the biblical account describes a scientific process both for the man and the woman. The woman's creation is from man and he is anesthetized. Ultimately, I theorize two ongoing infinite creations: Nature's gods/angels/white sperm/DNA and us from primitive man/black sperm/DNA. We are the mystery!

DNA similarities make world seem smaller

Survey says any two people 99.9 percent identical

By LEE BOWMAN
Scripps Howard News Service

Although everyone's genetic makeup is unique, scientists have found that populations from different parts of the world still share more genetic similarities than had been thought.

The results of a computer analysis of DNA from individuals representing 52 populations around the globe, published today in the journal *Science*, make up the largest such global survey of genetic diversity, and should help studies of ancient human migrations.

Those surveyed were broken into <u>five</u> regions: Africa, Eurasia, East Asia, Oceania and the Americas. Differences among individuals within those groups accounted for 93%-95% of genetic variety, according to the international team led by Marcus Feldman, a professor of humanities and sciences at Stanford University.

Compare the genetics of any two people, and the matchup will be about 99.9% identical. The research team accurately pinpointed the ancestral content of virtually every individual from Africa, East Asia, Oceania and the Americas. ■

---

1. How could Hopi medicine man know of five races, let alone the alien god? See illustration page (1).

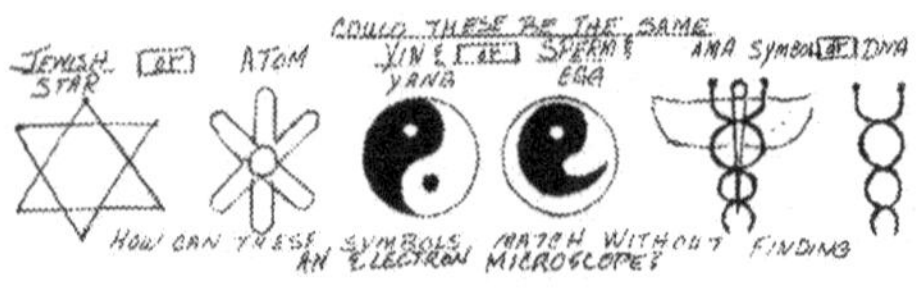

Alien statues found along banks of Jordan River 10,000 years old

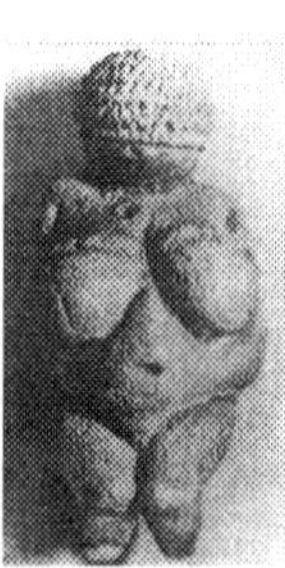

2. Notice alien head on mother goddess statue. This supports what gods look like in Genesis 6:4. Statue dated circa 5000 years old found in Jerusalem, Israel.

3. Notice asexual organs on alien statue. This confirms Yeshua's description of angels and explains why they don't give their hand in marriage.

Mother goddess statues represent the inevitable separation that was to occur. According to religion mankind is predestined. It happened because the "sons of gods" thought the daughters of men were pretty. Their "giant" offspring became men of great renown and all wickedness spread all over the earth. This exemplifies their lust for power due to their obvious oneness in looks and small size. And they must've considered themselves ugly. It took place during the mysterious time frame, of the last ice age approximately 13,000 years ago up to the beginning of the Jewish calendar, 4000 BC (6,000 years ago). These are found all over the earth. The alien headed one is from Israel circa 8000 years old. The round headed one is 30000 yrs. It is called the Venus of Willendorf. The asexual alien statue was found along the banks of the Jordan River. Notice the circles as if they knew about chromosomes and dna. These as all scientists agree were religiously important and found in every household. I theorize that like the pyramids and Easter Island giants they were left to stand the test of time to tell us what their gods look like and where they are, Aliens and space.

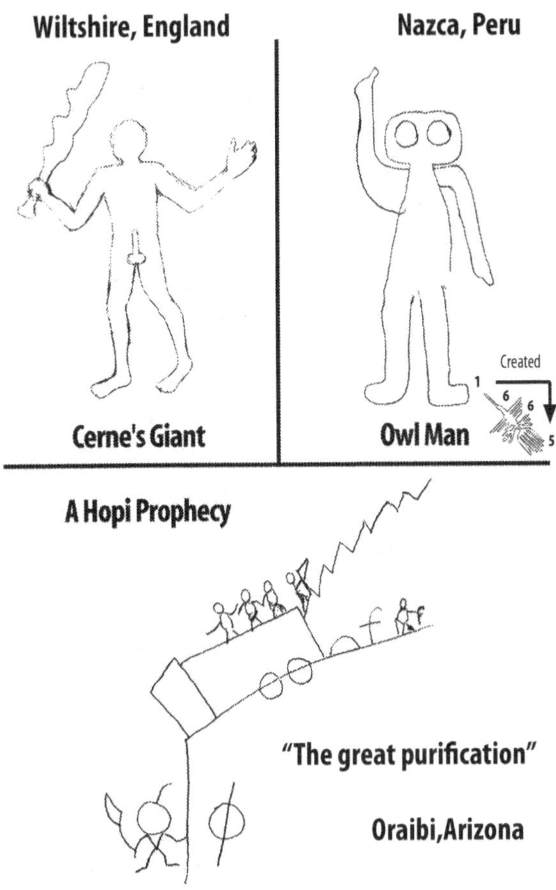

The Cerne's Giant tells us why they couldn't cohabitate with their creation of modern man (we kill for sex) and when they will return. (Three humps on club indicate an impending nuclear disaster. Atom has three parts.) The Owl man tells us where their gods live and what they look like, space and aliens. It has a hummingbird which represents fertility pointing at it. Count the appendages and see connection to biblical number of man 666 and five races. The Hopi prophecy again shows us an alien god (big headed guy) saving the earth from destruction and recycling the majority of man up, obviously to another planet. Again how did the shaman know of the five races of man let alone an alien God? Notice similarity of box carrier to today's truck trailer. Feather on head indicates gods' ability to fly. See saucer attached to his arm.

The Starchild controversy

SINCE FEBRUARY 1999 a bizarre looking skull, known as the Starchild skull, has been exhibited at UFO conferences and heavily discussed in UFO journals.

The Starchild skull is alleged to be the remains of an alien-human hybrid.

Legend of the Star People

According to the Starchild Project, an organization that wants to arrange DNA testing of the skull to prove an incredible origin, the skull was discovered in the mountains of northern Mexico. Indian tribes from the region have legends of Star People – beings from the sky who visit Earth to impregnate local women before returning years later to retrieve the hybrid infants.

A hybrid is a cross between two different breeds or species. Only closely related species can interbreed or "hybridize," and it seems unlikely that humans and aliens would be similar enough.

Big head

The skull has several strange features that suggest it is not human. It has a massive brain capacity, flattened rear, shallow eye sockets, and is missing the front sinuses.

The Starchild Project claims to have consulted over 50 experts, the vast majority of whom argue that the skull is that of a deformed human child.

Most experts say that the Starchild skull is that of a child suffering from hydrocephaly, a disease in which fluid builds up on the brain and makes the skull swell.

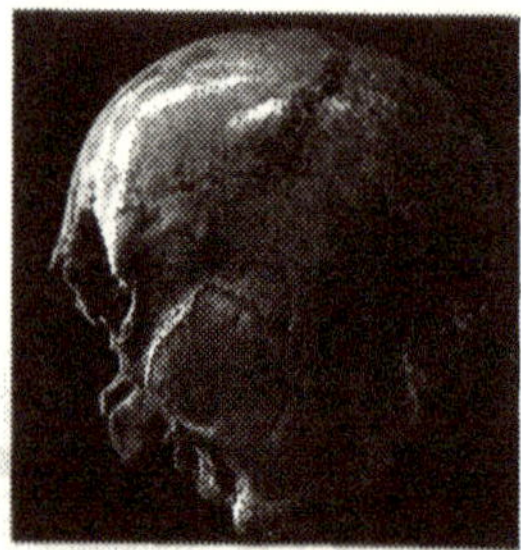

■ The Starchild skull *is far from normal. But is it from an abnormal or cradle-boarded human infant, or perhaps an alien-human hybrid?*

It is also widely thought that the skull has been cradle-boarded. Cradle-boarding is the practice of strapping an infant's head to a board and causes flattening of the back of the skull. It was practiced in the area of Mexico where the skull comes from. The Starchild Project argues that close examination of the skull rules out this explanation, and is attempting to raise funds to pay for DNA testing – the only way to be certain of the skull's origins.

"Beings from the sky" Is this the owl man? He is pointing up! This skull supports this. Also "impregnates women" supports the cover art of the mother goddess statue. Skull is evidence of aliens being flesh and blood and these "sons of God" in Genesis 6:4. It supports my theory that they are not religious "spirit" magical beings. However, I conclude the atom, which makes everything, is "religion's invisible spirit" creator, evolving scientifically through time, not by magic. Read on.

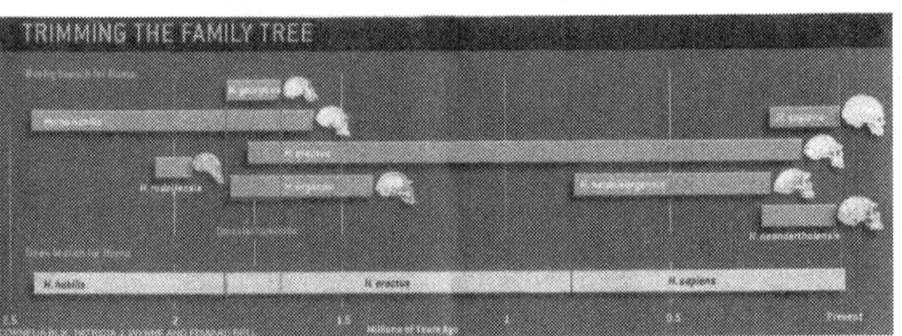

The alien skull shows the obvious mix between primitive man and himself producing us. We are the mystery! This is supported by a missing link. There isn't any fossil between the laid back forehead and our upright one. Notice the lack of brow on the alien skull and our extremely reduced one now. Duh! This and our overly large head make it abundantly clear that we are the scientific missing link. We didn't evolve we were scientifically created by manipulating natures perfect creation, primitive man.(look at yin and yang symbol) I propose two ongoing infinite creations of man, natures primitive man(black sperm) and modern man's by the aliens/us (white sperm). There is a biblical reference to us being called mystery and the number 666. However, religion makes it the devil, even though it is a feminine reference. Anyway, this means modern man is infinitely doomed to be separate from their heavenly existence of space travel and life. The scripture even makes reference to us as female and the serpent of old. "Fugitive Serpent" science confuses the mother-goddess statues for a belief that god is female. I theorize it represents the alien god mixing with the pretty daughters of man. This is possible with DNA and supported by serpent worship. It is further supported by universal serpent worship and symbols all over the earth. The whore reference indicates reincarnation and a continual lust for sexual beauty. The aliens are the father. Mankind's body is the mother! That's the reason I put the quote "Come up out of her my people" on the back cover by Yeshua. It is also why the term "mother of abominations" was ap plied to mankind. My second book goes into great detail about this duality of the alien body. Hell, we are dual, too. We have x and y chromosomes and the symbols come from the tenth planet. They match sperm and an egg like an arrow and target. Macrocosm science! The Alien statue from the banks of the Jordan River is asexual. The biblical devil is feminine. It is the voice in our head. This is the reason for doing the mystery and "killing" it and why it talked to eve instead of Adam. Read on! The return to our first body is scientific. Mankind/religion's devil is an illusion. He is called that which "Isn't", but was and will be again thrown into the lake of fire. This is the earth, universe's prison for another lake of fire/burning desire, us.

"Serpent of old, mystery, the whore, Mother, that which isn't, was and will be mankind 666!"

Giants of Easter Island South Pacific

Notice the saucer on top of head tells us where they live just like owl man, aboriginal god, and Starchild legend spaceships just like front covers. Six strands of rock looks like DNA readouts. It also could implicate the sixth chromosome mystery or the Jewish creation on the sixth day. Giants were the offspring of gods and "pretty" daughters of man. This is when our separation occurred because wickedness spread all over the earth. A great flood followed. This is a red figure that symbolized mankind. See how he is doing the mystery or transcendental meditation.

The six strands of rock below the Alien looking god could symbolize a DNA readout. I am intrigued by it being six strands. The day of man's biblical creation is the 6th. The Hopi prophecy has six beings (five of man, one of an alien). The hummingbird of the owl man in Nazca reflects this theme as does the biblical "devil". Is it possible that the sixth chromosome is the source of this "looks' manipulation. I've been reading a fascinating book called "The Sixth Chromosome". There are many other things pointing to creation involving the number six like the atom and Jewish star's number of points. The planet mars is the sixth from the tenth. There's more read on! Also, look at man meditating/doing mystery. He is made of red lava rock and is similar to many other representations of first religious worship. Red also represents blood and creation. Mystery worship is universal from Buddhism to sitting Indian style. (See statue of Indian from Tennessee at end of book) Also notice black moai that looks somewhat different from the whiter standing ones. This parallels black and white yin and yang. It also parallels Mayan statues on next page.

This is religion's game of Olmecs from Mexico. They are also known for mysterious carvings of huge heads!

 Figure circled is made of red lava rock like Easter Island man doing mystery. This is what power struggle of gods is about, us. Red symbolizes creation. Notice opposing sides black and white like Easter Island Man and Yin and Yang. Notice six obelisks like stones. Coincidence? Don't think so. Notice similarities to Easter Island statues, Israel statues, aborigines, all other "big headed" God statues from every continent.

The figures are all black and white "facing" each other. The one in the back that is porous looking is the only red one. Could this represent the power struggle over mankind's inevitable creation and does it involve the sixth chromosome? Also, notice the clear resemblance to the alien statue from Israel and the head on the mother goddess statue as well. It clearly looks like the Easter Island heads except for the elongation. They are the product of the mix between the sons of gods/aliens and man. I think losing the bulbous head was the first indicator of their pursuit toward outward beauty. The story supports this with their reason for mixing in the first place. (See back cover)

The bronze statue is from Kiev and is circa 8000 years old. It has six fingers supporting the existence and authenticity of the Roswell Alien autopsy. The recovered dead alien had six fingers and toes. This figure also supports the need for gold as protection in space. It has a Halo. Compare it to the following aboriginal gods. They look alien and even have gold painted halos around their heads. The Aztec block shows two hands intertwined with six fingers. These hands alone represent their god's creation of them and the entanglement represents D.N.A., how they were created. These match our medical symbol, intertwined serpents. How can they match when it takes an electron microscope to see them? The gods must be scientifically advanced!

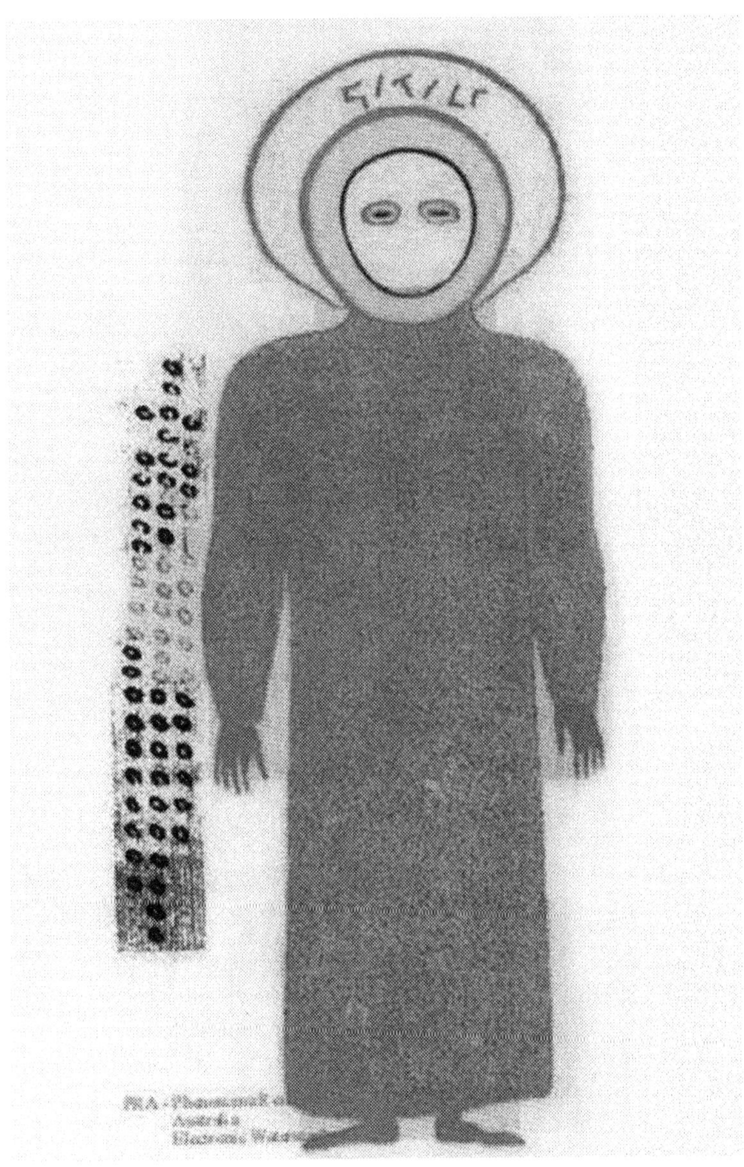

Aborigine cave drawing dated circa 30000 years old. Notice hieroglyphics on gold halo. See more on following page. Also notice readout similar to Easter Island one .These rock layouts/DNA readouts are common across the earth.

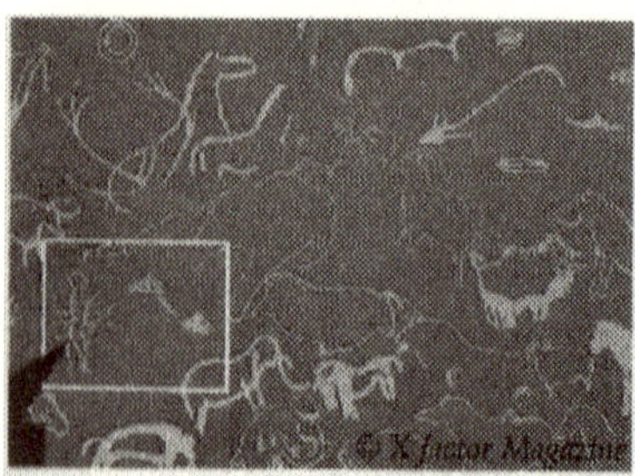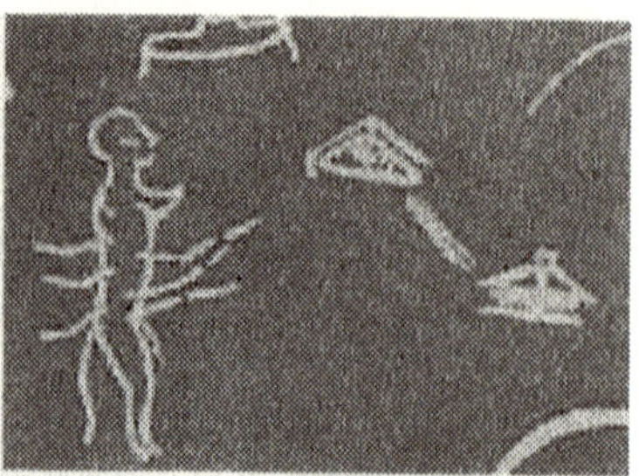

Japanese discovery on the island now known as Taiwan. It is a drawing by a general that discovered a strange ship on the island. This happened in 1806! Notice the ships drawn above it. He found this drawing on the hull of the ship. The writing looks like the hieroglyphics found on the aboriginal gods halo and supports the description of Roswell's.

The cave art clearly shows matching saucers. This is dated circa 15000 years old. It is in France. It shows smaller ships coming out of a large one and abduction! The lines represent the invisible energy taking the human up. The top right picture is the oldest rock of aliens from Africa date circa 50000 yrs. old. It shows the little alien/Roswell gray in control observing. He's even protected by a box that looks much like a tree trimmer's carriage. The others are larger and restraining one of their own. They must have first made themselves larger to be more able to control their scientific manipulations of primitive man. They are obviously serving the little guy and they are struggling with one of their own. Anyway, this supports the scientific manipulation of themselves. See the one with the horns. Is this what gave us the first images of the biblical "devil". Read on! See similarity to statues on following page.

These reptilian looking skulls are found in Ubaid Iraq. They look like the reptilian look-ing tall ones on the rock art of the previous page. Scientists have repeatedly mistaken the eyes for sunglasses or goggles. However they are very similar to the large slanted eyes of the Roswell gray alien. They are identical to the eyes of the mother goddess statue from Israel. Notice one is a divided looking skull, giving it the appearance of hornlike appendages, while the other is elongated. They are clearly two different types. Were these a product of the first attempts to make themselves larger for power or for mining gold. Anyway, it is clear here and in the writings that scientific creation was producing things like this, the mothman, centaur and other abnormalities. The little guy with a HUGE head is from Utah! See appendages (Devil's horns?).

Three famous U.F.O. incidents in the U.S. reported on the front page of each respective city's newspaper. The dates and places are on the last two. The first is Los Angeles and shows us shooting at it. It happened in Feb. 25, 1942. No wonder they don't cohabitate with us. We never recovered it.

286 **GENESIS REVISITED**

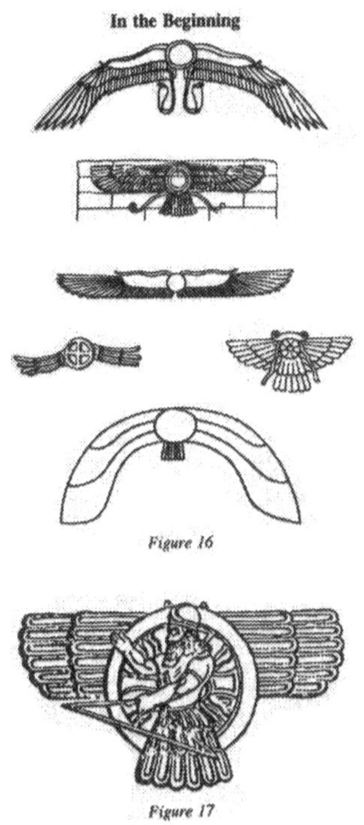

Figure 16

Figure 17

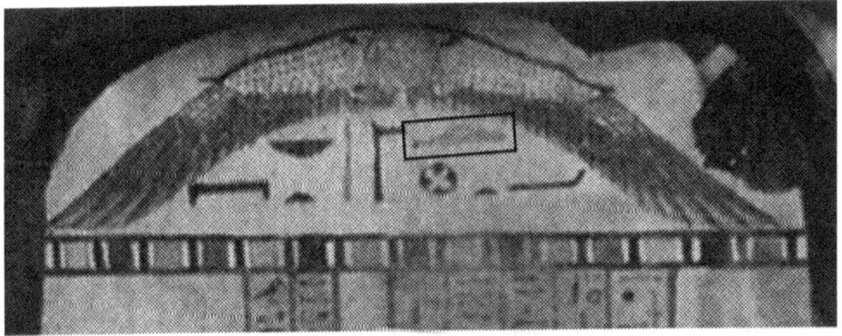

These are all ancient symbols for god from Sumeria, Babylonia, Assyria, to the Egyptian one at the bottom. It has an actual saucer below the omni-present symbol of god which could literally be called a flying saucer. They all share this characteristic! Now we know why they're everywhere. But remember the atom is also a circle that is "every-thing". The Egyptian god is Atum! Notice the snakes for DNA creation. Also notice the cross symbol. It is the oldest geometry on earth representing the 10th planet. The Assyrian one clearly shows how man put himself in the circle. He became god!

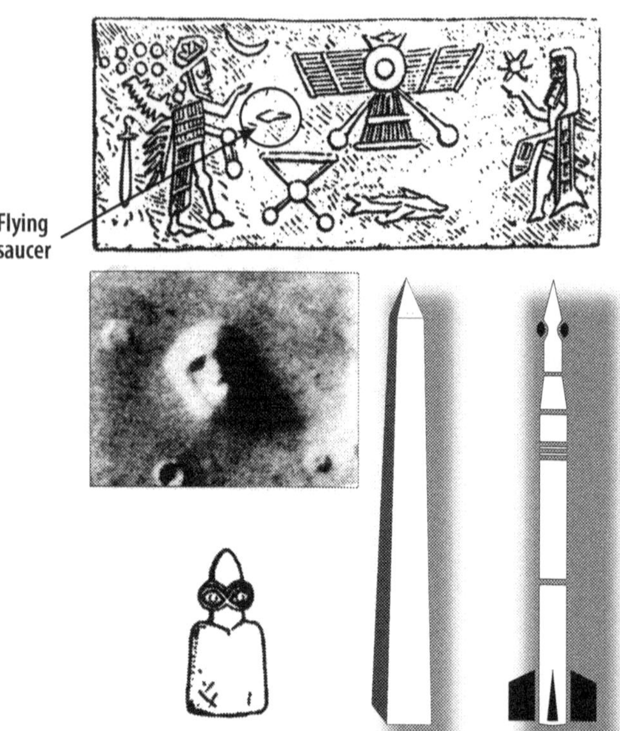

1. Notice the satellite on the clay tablet going from Earth (7th planet) to Mars (6th planet). It looks just like ones today. This tablet is also circa 13000 years. Also notice symbol for Mars matches atom and jewish star. Is this proof that Mars could have had Man there first and we destroyed it with nuclear weapons? The "man" on mars is in a suit. Is it reason for contact?

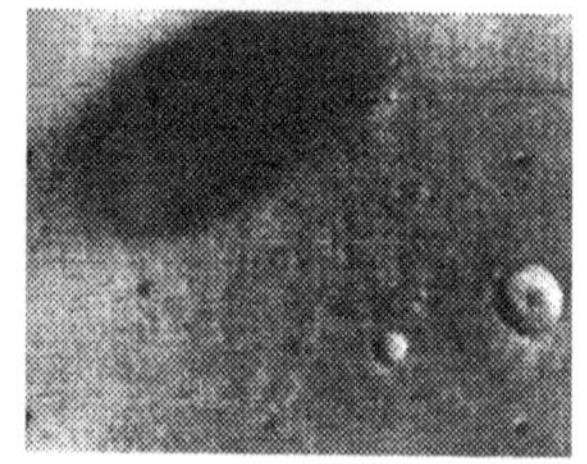

2. See how the helmet of Mars "man" matches our pictures of face on Mars.

3. Notice ancient satellite looks like alien head and eyes of nuclear missile. Egyptian obelisk matches nuclear missile. Egyptians called obelisks shem "rocketship".

4. See flying saucer monitoring earth on mars clay tablet.

5.This is a photo from phobos satellite sent to view mars moon phobos. It is irregular shaped and appears to be hollow. Could it be used as a space base on the inside? We think asteroids could be used this way as natural spaceships. This is the last picture it took before it was deemed "destroyed" by space debris. Looks like a flying saucer to me.

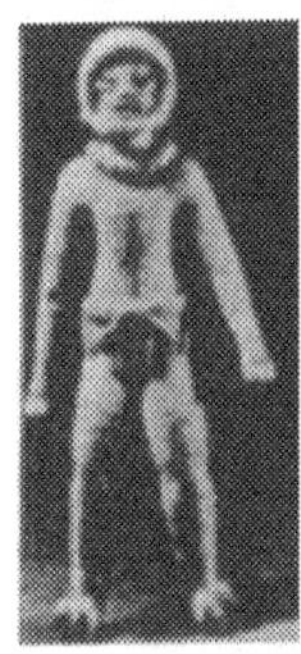
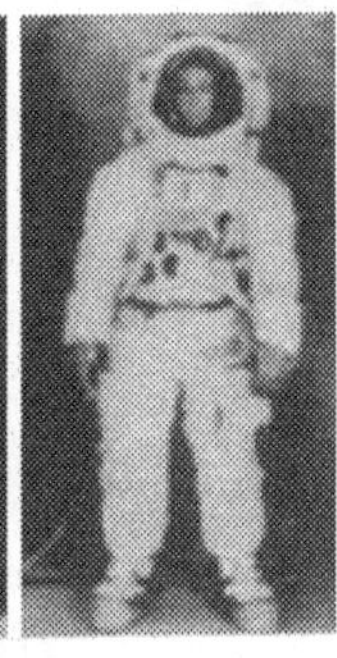
This evidence speaks for itself. These are ancient astronaut statues compared to a real one. The bottom one is identical. It was found in Peru and is 6000 years old.

Also, these are airplane statues found in ... They are made of solid gold. This support space travels need for gold and proves gods are flesh and blood beings who have already conquered space!

THESE SPEAK FOR THEMSELVES AS WELL. They are all made of gold. From Egypt to Peru!

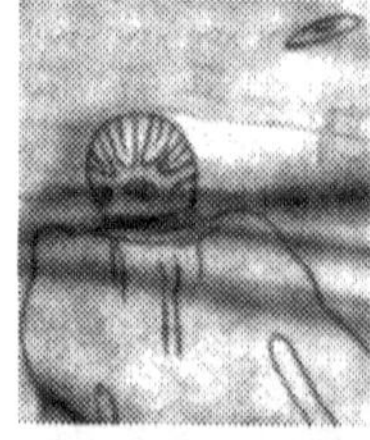

Cave
Astronaut

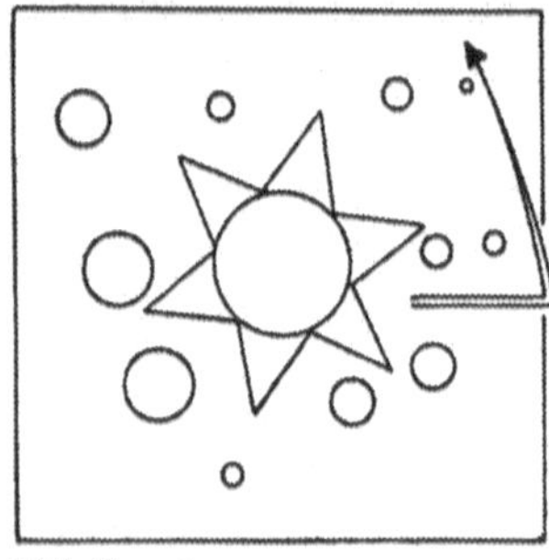

10th Planet

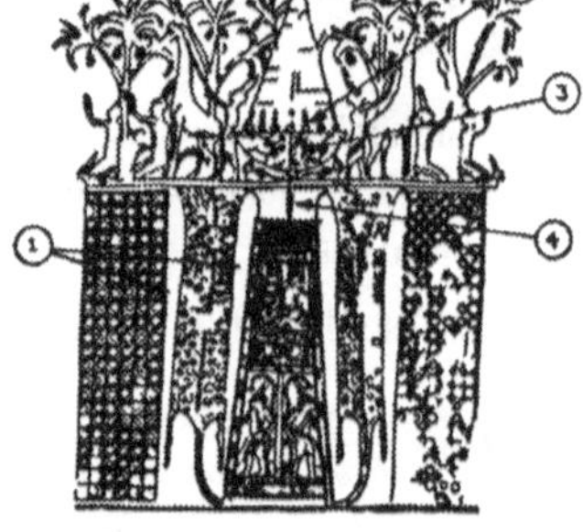

1. Notice cave grid looks like computer grid of space. Also star of cave sculpture just like the Sumerian clay tablet below. The clay tablet is dated circa 13000 years. The cave drawing is much older. They both show a 10th planet in our solar system. HOW?

2. The cave astronaut and gemini-looking capsule are also ancient. This is proof they existed before and supports my conclusion. Read on!

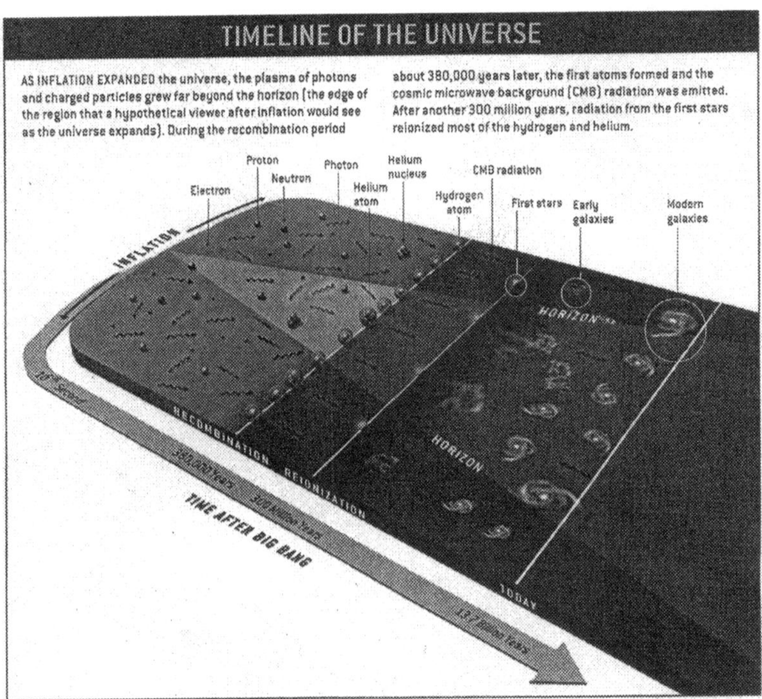

This is a perfect example of macrocosm science. The smallest parts mirror the whole. Atoms, photons, solar systems galaxies all resemble the universe itself. The ancient geometry supports this theory/reality. I was amazed at how much a woman's egg looks like the sun (magnified) and when the sperm penetrates it the outer shell grows a green growth that becomes the placenta. The earth would only grow green vegetation from photon penetration. Photons look like sperm. Atoms look like suns, these look like eggs! Anyway, The problem with a beginning to our universe is that it is infinite. Only matter has a "beginning and ending". But this is an oxy-moron because atoms make matter and though one form ends it doesn't stop existing, another one just begins. This is all about image! Mind over matter and to be free of matters constraints we must free ourselves from the matter. For space travel/freedom it is literally what we have to do. Free ourselves from the inevitable invisible eater of matter. GRAVITY! Matter itself. Does all this really matter? To be free it does. Flying is the ultimate freedom!

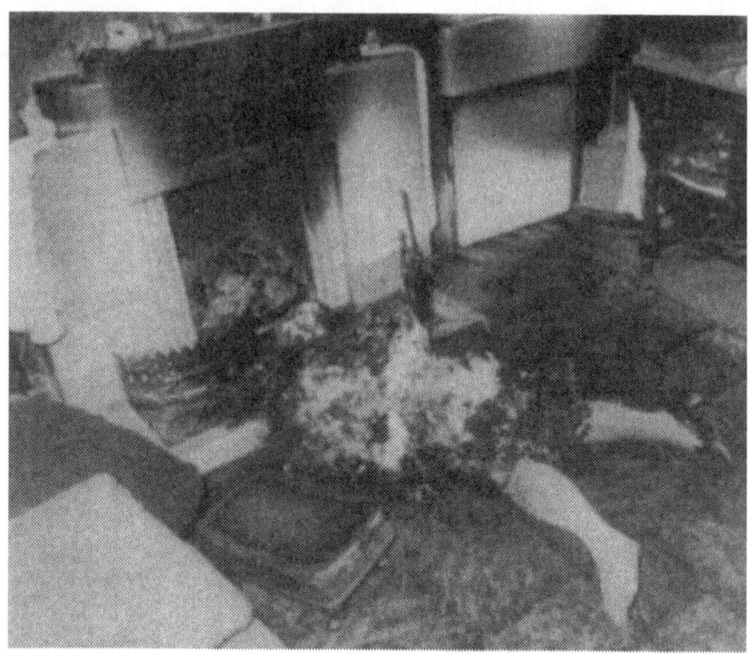

 Just thought I'd throw this one in to show you proof of nuclear fusion/fission by atoms. We are made of atoms. Adams are atoms. If you think you know everything you better think again. This is a spontaneous human combustion victim. The feet are left to possibly drive home my point about flying and who we truly are! This is a perfect reason to start seeking the kingdom of Heaven! Knowledge of the Universe.

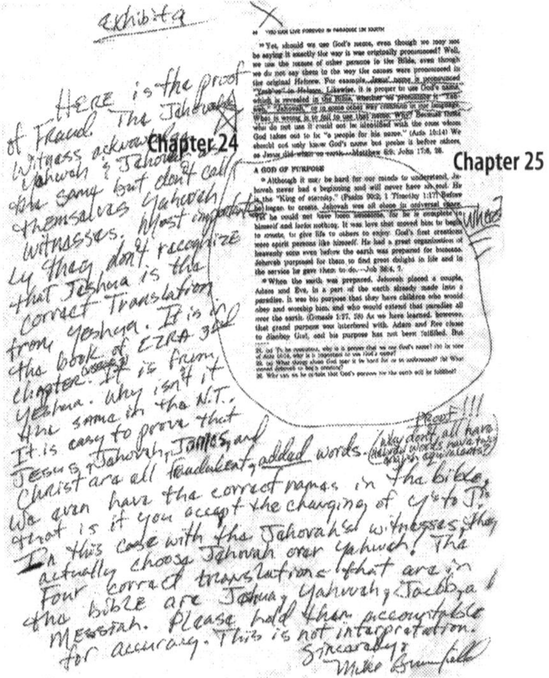

1. "Where is God?" is the $64,000 question. I thought God is omnipresent! That means everywhere like the atom! They say he's all alone in space!

2. They say he's not lonesome but he's all alone. Then they say he creates for others. That's loneliness.

3. Finally they say he creates a heavenly organization of "spirit" sons like "himself". Why not daughters? And now they skip the fall of the angels story.

4. Last but not least. This is the proof that "religion". At least the Jews make these angels and god "spirit" not flesh and blood. This is the ultimate cover-up. What if they come back and are the aliens? WWYD?

5. Proof that the J.W.'s discredit science! And ironically the scripture above James 2:9 makes their god a hypocrite. He has a favorite, yet forbids it. The chosen race of the Jews. No wonder people revere the Jews!

6. Finaly they say the "Devil" is working through the U.N.! Don't they want a United Earth?

Last but certainly not least! These are dropa stones from Tibet and are circa10000 years old. They were found deep in a cave with the remains of about 400 skeletons of little people with big heads. The island of Khafu values an identical stone as money. They are called money stones. The largest ones measure up to 10 feet, and are made of polished white limestone. The whiter they are the more valuable. Now we see where the white thing comes from in religion. If these gods stay in spaceships they would be really white looking. The universal alien is the Roswell gray! If you don't buy this then buy an alien doll. It will be him!

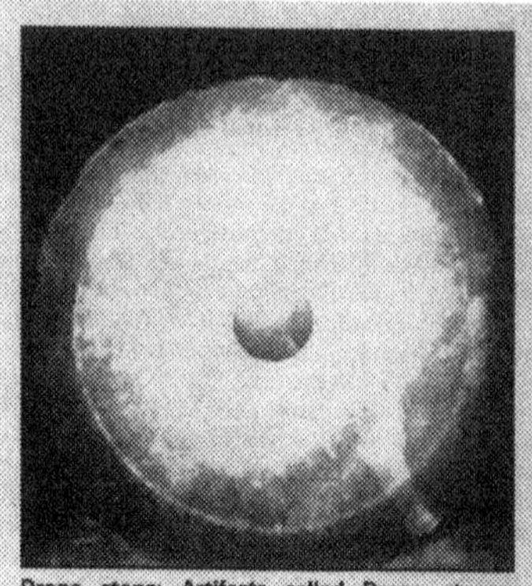

Dropa stone: Artifacts called Dropa stones, which bear an uncanny resemblance to the UFOs involved in the tether incident.

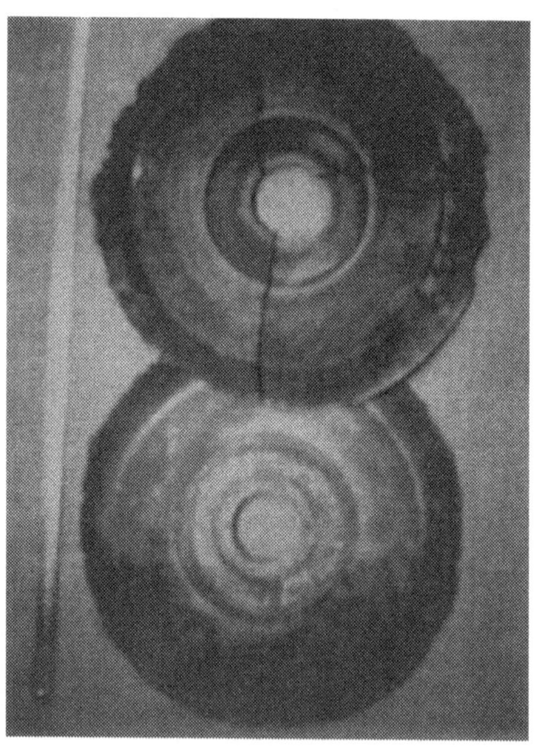

THE
TWO WITNESSES
AND
THE
Religion
DISCOVER THIS
SHOCKING BIBLE
PROPHECY IN
REVELATION!
BY MICHAEL
WARNING: SOLVING THIS MYSTERY MAY BE HARMFUL TO YOUR HEALTH!

The Future Alien Contact

INTRODUCTION

Read *The Future Alien Contact*. This is "my" final story of research into mankind's origins. It is a fiction, based on real events and actual scientific discoveries. Some of the characters are real as well.

It ALL began, with a mysterious dream, in 1989. The dream was about my future! Much to my disbelief, this dream became a reality. It came to fruition, twelve years later, through my best-selling book; *The Two Witnesses and the Religion Cover-up.*

It's true! Everybody does love a good mystery. Although, "good" is relative in this story. Actually, that's what the cover-up is all about. This creation of man. Isn't it obvious we aren't any good? I put a warning at the bottom of the front cover. It reads "Warning: Solving this mystery may be harmful to your health."

The Future Alien Contact

Seemingly, fate brought me to Nashville, Tennessee. But, from the beginning, I had an eerie realization that the dream was coming true. I didn't believe in fate, until then. However, this was my dream! Now, I believe anything is possible. Well, except for blinking thinking magic. This never changed.

A friend of mine, living in Nashville, asked me to come down and do a chainsaw exhibition. We are both from Ohio. I'm an artist and specialize in wooden Indians so this sounded like a great idea. He owned a new satellite business and was pursuing a country music career. I wanted to start playing guitar and sing. I had always loved singing in church. This was my "golden" opportunity. Or was it "ours"? I did write a best-selling book as a result of this "chance" encounter. Timing is "everything." Well I came, but soon "destiny" revealed a very different path for us. One that inevitably became a very rough and rocky road! I ended up staying and we began a journey of discovery. It would change our lives, forever.

We embarked on a turbulent search for the "spiritual" truth of mankind's origin. Where did we come from and what happened to religion? How did one become so many? Boy, what an adventure it was, and at the end, we aren't together anymore! Our spiritual pursuit would end with "my" discovery of alien evidence by primitive man. It didn't take place until the end of the first book. In the beginning, I believed that we are spirits. Hell, all religions do, so why not me—I was raised religious. I believed this, because of my buddy's out-of-body experience and the universal theme of being born again. He relentlessly pressed this issue and two scriptures by Jesus: "You must be born again of the water and the spirit" and "Flesh and blood shall not enter the kingdom of Heaven." He said that this body is water and he didn't have a body when he was outside of himself. I believed him. I still do. However, I have found no proof, ancient or otherwise, of the spirit existence.

But I soon discovered a universal theme among OBE victims. They are moving and this freaks them out. "Moving" became a key element of my research. Where were they going? Could we have another body, what Jesus called a "glorified" body? The ancient artwork supported this reality.

THE FUTURE ALIEN CONTACT

Hang on, because you're about to have the "Time" of your life.

The first book evolved into a trilogy. I didn't plan it. It just happened. The first and second books have three chapters. I didn't plan that, either. This book only has one, "The Future Alien Contact," and it solves the enigma of time itself. I have always been fascinated by religion's god/gods/angels not having time. I read all the Greek "myths" I could. They are depicted as men and women. This led to "my" speculation that the gods were physical beings. Why would spirits create physical beings, anyway. They created mankind. The word *creation* pointed me toward science, not magic. I felt, they must've created us for something they didn't want to do. But what about this soul/spirit world that my buddy and all religion believe in? This question and its answers will clear up the "moving" experience of the OBE victims and our possible glorified body. Is it an alien? Is this the reason we are seeing spaceships? Is our real body on one?

Anyway, back to our reason for being created: hard work immediately comes to mind. Nobody likes it! "My" first connection to this theory and them is gold. It is the oldest evidence in our mystery. Digging gold is hard work and every primitive culture was doing it, for them! Why? Gold is a common theme among religion and Adam was a "tiller of the ground." This begs us to question, "Why would 'magic spirit' gods need gold?"

And yes, there is a conflict in religion, about the number of gods. Judaism and its successors are the only monotheistic religion and their god is invisible! All others are polytheistic and real! I will attempt to explain this, and how religion's trinity correlates to space, matter, and time. These three fundamental scientific concepts make up the mystery of the universe. "I" propose to have solved the mystery of mankind in the first book, but not these. This is extremely complicated. They are "like" one, dependent upon each other, and part of an infinite universe with infinite possibilities. It is called macrocosm science.

I researched quantum physics and began seeing scientific parallels to confusing religious doctrines. I saw that "most" could be explained scientifically. Ancient art looks like today's science. For example, the two trees in the Garden of Eden sound like DNA. It matches the ancient AMA symbol! And it sure has opened our eyes, like it did Adam's and Eve's, to a whole new world. That is if there is an Adam and Eve. A world of creation possibilities through science, not "spirit magic." Please remember this! Creation is a crucial element of "my" conclusion. So is their biblical command to only eat from "one" tree. It involves our addiction to sex and beauty. And they do rule mankind. Variety "is" the spice of life. They are our problem.

Back to my scientific theory! Trinity also sounds like the three stages of matter and time. Could they have conquered time and science? If ancient man gave us religious symbols and traditions matching today's science, then isn't it possible that these gods are flesh and blood scientific beings? Could they have conquered space because of their oneness in looks? And lack of outward beauty. They do have the desire for mankind's pretty daughters. Why else would they think of them as pretty? The heads of Easter Island support this theory (see picture on back cover). They are the giants, the offspring of this union between the gods and pretty daughters of man. The aliens are small!

Isn't it possible that we are the most destructive creation in the universe, because of our differences. This would support predestination and their torturous absence, if we are infinite beings. We must cure ourselves. And in predestination there are no coincidences. Primitive man's religion does teach that man's destiny is already known. Are we beauty addicts and do we have deja vu?

Religion's story is universally common. I will simplify it using the Jewish story. Yeshua is a Jew and the most famous man on earth. He was conceived through the "immaculate" conception. This again makes man evil because it means by "god". "He" is immortal, omni-present, and it goes without saying Omnipotent. Where is the scripture to support this claim? I don't know! Sounds like the atom. The J.W.'s make him an individual saying he's somewhere in the universe.(see evidence) However, there are many scripture supporting his omni-presence meaning everywhere. This would mean he is the universe. Then he creates immortal spirit angels. How do you create immortality? Atoms are immortal and can't be created or destroyed. The J.W.'s say they're like himself and just son's, but this makes them omni-present, too. (Why not the daughters and how do you create a spirit?) Where is their creation story? There isn't any! Why not? Read on! "One-third" are thrown out, because of one saying he can be more powerful than god. (Why not half?) Right! "He" challenges god and lives with "him"? This "angel leader" becomes religion's devil. I thought they were all equal. Is this when hell is "created"? This is the obvious mystery. Is man created before or after? The J.W.'s say after. (see evidence) The story goes in Genesis that man was created "immortal". How? He is at least carbon based, being made from the ground. But he's made in god's image! This is a big problem, because image is form. God's everywhere and invisible, which means spirit! Eve is made from Adam, which sounds like science and we finally got a woman thing happening. Now, the mystery becomes simple. The "woman" falls prey to the devil and they are driven out of the garden/paradise. The devil isn't mentioned anymore and they start multiplying. Why? That's when the "other" (which ones, good or bad) angels start seeing their daughters as pretty and have sex with them. How does a spirit have sex? They begat giants and they become great men of reknown, sounds like a power thing. This is when wickedness spread all over the earth and god wiped them out with a flood. He forbid this ever again. Could these two separations be one and the same? "Mankind" tries to get "back" to paradise/heaven with the tower of babel and this is "supposedly" how we got our different looks and languages. God stopped us and then confused us by doing this. Huh, sounds like a good way to keep us ignorant. Last, but not least, there will be a second coming to save us from ourselves. This takes place because of a global event that could destroy the Earth. I propose that this could be a nuclear war. It is supported by the following evidence!

Now, back to my evidence! The atom, which also has three components, geometrically matches the Jewish star. Coincidence? I didn't think so. Read on! The Jewish story deals with my name as well. I put these on the back cover of every book, and only my first name on the front! I saw that all ancient art was geometrical and matched today's science. I also thought that today's religious traditions (same as primitive man's) mimicked future technologies:

teleportation/disappearing, holograms/spirit, anti-gravity/levitation. I was fast becoming a scientist, but my buddy wasn't. It just happened. It was my evolution, from ignorance to scientific knowledge. Knowledge is power.

My parents' religion, the Jehovah's Witnesses, wanted to keep me ignorant. They said, "All other religions were from the Devil." Man, I thought to myself, religion had a sure fire method of brainwashing you. They said everyone else is wrong! I laughed when I thought about the First Jewish Commandment "Thou shalt have no other gods before me." Duh! Hell, they all had gods! Man created a new disease. It's mental and is called self-righteousness. I left them and went to college. College rhymes with knowledge. I began to study Albert Einstein. He gave us the theory of relativity. His theory indicates time is relative and conquerable, which means time really doesn't exist. Religion confirmed this, for the gods/god/angels, anyway. The Aliens did too. If these beings exist, then couldn't time travel be happening now? Man is the time dweller. Isn't that the same as time traveling? Religion and the aliens agree upon reversing time.

Science is also confirming this possibility. Yeshua is the messenger! This is my point about coincidences.

Read on! The first book examines the sixty-four-thousand-dollar question, "Is there life out there?" Since we were both "raised/brainwashed" as Christians, we started there. Please read on and find out why these could be the same. Do the angels and god/gods really exist? Why didn't people look for ancient evidence of them? We started with our common denominator of life, religion, and we know the quote by Frederick Nietzsche that it is "the opiate of the masses." It's a drug used to keep you from looking elsewhere, like the First Jewish Commandment. We knew this, but like time, it is also a universal theme of primitive man. This is important! There are many others like "GOLD"! This is the most important. Read on.

We already knew religion's answer, though. It was taught to us all our lives. But, we were never taught science. Our parents believed in a "spirit god" from Heaven that created us. Again, why would spirits create flesh beings? Created sounded like science and not magic. And ironically Heaven was universally "up." Why would "spirits" come from "up" and why would they "create" us. Why not just speak us into existence as it says in the book of Job? The Jewish creation story says we were created from the dust of the ground. Eve was created from Adam's ribs like cloning! And why do these contradict each other? This is important! It became the simplest, and most crucial, evidence in solving our mystery. "Up-ness" is absolutely irrefutable. Look at front cover!

Last but not least, how did spirits come to be; how do they live and why would they create flesh beings? Not to mention, how does a spirit breed with us? We found more problems. Our parents' God is immortal and first creates immortal angels. How do you create something that is immortal? This is a contradiction. Secondly, where is the angel creation story? And forget about asking them where "God" came from. They told us that it requires blind faith, to just accept that "he" is everywhere and nothing "created" "Him." We felt like the blind following the blind.

Wow! I suddenly realized something remarkable. We create things and science theorizes that time travel is possible. And we know that the universe is infinite. Could we be created and yet infinite? This had to be about time travel! The wheels were turning and I was on to something. Could other people from an older planet be visiting us? Could we be visiting ourselves from the future? I had to know. No. I already knew. Ancient Alien evidence was on every continent! I knew that religion came from primitive man. Primitive meant ignorant. Having been a history major in college, with a minor in business, I didn't buy swamp land in Florida. With all the ancient evidence, I theorized that our creation was scientific. Primitive man must've created this magic "spirit" factor of religion, due to his ignorance. The matching symbols and my own scientific ignorance of cloning and genetics was enough for me. This is possible!

And last but not least: the lack of magic. It doesn't exist! *Genes* sounded like *genesis* and *atom* sounded like *Adam*. And now, I have discovered the Egyptian god is Atum. Wow! What an unbelievable "coincidence." Wait till you read all the others I found.

The manipulation of our genes will affect us

all. It all starts here and can possibly end here. Science theorizes that it will conquer our aging dilemma. It is already turning the tide on disease. Think about the wonderful future of scientific achievements, for our children, if religion doesn't kill us all first. But, then again, this is all about time travel through living in a primitive state of mankind. This reality fueled my search even more. The universe is infinite and our possibilities are too! Adams (mankind) are made of atoms, like the rest of the universe. This is the basis of quantum physics and macrocosm science. Could we be a mirror image of the universe?

Back to my point about our first book, *The Two Witnesses and the Religion Cover-up*. Religion came from primitive man, and his magic "spirit" teaching entrenched the world. It still prevails today and is taught exactly the same way. It is outdated. We must update it and remove this religious "veil" of ignorance. Women's, too! It's a scientific world and that's a fact! Their self-righteous magic god and cruel barbaric traditions sickened me. I'm sorry, but I can't understand this religious mentality. We should be a scientific world. There isn't one of us that would reject a scientific cure for death except for religious fanatics, and this is sad. Doesn't the world have enough misery and suffering, without religion inflicting more? And, if that's not bad enough, the universe is riddled with flying debris. This made their "perfect" god seem even more ridiculous. It is ruled by utter chaos and always threatening our existence! This should be enough to make us challenge religion's perfect God and perfect universe.

I often think about our fragileness. I certainly understood the "Golden Rule" now. Age was helping me. Our youth is nothing but foolishness. Before, I didn't think there was a reason for anything, other than sexual/ego selfishness. Now, I know better. All of my wrongdoings/"mistakes" stemmed from this fact alone. I didn't want to hurt anybody else! This became my "reason" to continue. I don't mean to be so hard on religion but children don't deserve religious persecution. I started challenging them all. My siblings and I didn't deserve it. Religious parents strip their children of religious freedom. They also oppress their ability to learn about science and the world around them. Most religions resist science, even though science is making huge strides. It is also constantly restrained by religious politicians. This is sad because our world has become global and science could make "real" miracles happen. Children die at the hands of religious parents every day, even though science could save them. I saw it, many times, in my ex-religion and it is still happening. I wanted to ban religion, or make preachers heal sick children. If they can't, then spirit magic obviously doesn't exist.

I don't agree with the need for religion. We need scientific freedom. We have the law to make us "be" good. Doesn't this make it obvious that we are a flawed creation? Scientifically sex and different looks don't mix. Religion creates wars and killers. We must recognize this side effect. It is a global disease. This is a scientific fact of life! We've had war ever since god/gods/sons of God (angels) left and religion began. (I use all these titles because in the first book we examined all religions.) Actually, I found that we had it when they were here with us, too! Obviously, it all started with our creation. Maybe, the war in "Heaven" was about our creation.

This is my final question. Are we a really

"good" product/creation? I ask this because, after all, they had a perfect world and God even foresaw our hell. Come on, I mean really let's think about it. In the Bible's beginning (which is the story of man's creation and not the angels; where is the angel story?) Heaven and Earth are one! Earth must've become man's prison. But! It is a fragile paradise and we are its worst enemy. This can't be. It is illogical and ridiculous.

Let's solve this mystery. The majority of the world is ruled by the Jewish calendar and religion. It is only six thousand years old. That is not very long ago! We should have, at the very least, a few million years of history. What am I saying? We should have infinite knowledge, be traveling throughout the universe, and creating new Earths! This was made famous by the Drake Equation. That Earth has happened everywhere. They are paradise! Living in a spaceship would get old, quick. It's an insult to my intelligence to think that I couldn't solve our mystery. Six thousand years is such a short time. I looked for the simplest answers.

This is the most sacred rule of science called Occam's Razor. If planets and every living thing beneath us doesn't think/create, then look for the simplest answer. Planet Earth must exist now, and before, and again. Now, let's look at the facts about us. We are still very primitive and driven by three things: power, sex and survival. And really, it's all about sex. That's obvious. (See Cernes Giant inside pictures.) That's how primitive we really are. I knew we made a lot of mistakes in their pursuit. I did. So did President Clinton! I wrote about this in my first book. I write about President Bush in this one. Not for sexual innuendos, but for religious hypocrisy. He kills instead of turning the other cheek, but he's a Christian.

Our search began to uncover, many older cultures, than the Jews. We even found that the Jewish Bible is a collection of books and not one story. What! My ex-religion says it is one story, "the perfect story." It was canonized/edited by powerful murderous Jewish Kings. No way! This is ridiculous, but it was true. I discovered my ex-religion was lying to me. Their God even kills his children when he doesn't have to. He foresaw it. I couldn't buy this magic perfectionist not being a perfectionist. And he's cruel, too!

We became more determined than ever to solve this mystery. Just maybe there are older books than Moses. Since we were "raised/brainwashed" to believe in Jesus we started there. After all he is the most famous man in the world!

This quickly led to my shocking discovery of a Jewish prophecy and contact. Wow, it solves the mystery of mankind! I went straight to it using a concordance. I like to cut to the chase. Why didn't everybody do this? Then I realized something, I just recently became a "seeker"! The Bible was confusing and I couldn't stomach its killing god! In this prophecy the mystery is solved and time is no more. This seemed logical if time is relative. But much to my dismay the answer tortures mankind. This didn't seem logical! Why would it torture us? I got a nagging suspicion. My scientific approach was beginning to torture my partner, friends, and family. This nagging suspicion supported my theory about how these gods/angels could've had a perfect existence. I only saw "one" way if we all looked the same. The Easter Island heads supports this theory. (See picture inside.) Surprisingly the prophecy involves two men like my buddy and me. Man, this is weird. Somehow I didn't think this was a coincidence. Our struggle definitely mirrored the world's science versus religion, alien versus spirit! This scared me because they get killed. If it is us and I didn't take that too seriously I found relief in the following scripture. "They are resurrected in front of the world." They are resurrected by…! "What Michael the archangel?" This is contact! Wow could it be? How could I be him and one of the two witnesses too? But was I either? What am I talking about, we are all here in the end anyway. I thought about the quote on the back cover of my second book.

Read on and discover how this is a logical sequence of events and why I could be both! But it doesn't make me special if I am. In fact I'm not! We're all equal! Michael follows their resurrection. He doesn't perform it! This is important. He reveals the angels! Wow! I saw aliens in my dream and thought it was crazy just like everyone else. Well, not everyone. I soon discovered plenty of people with a similar experience. But the alien ugliness bothered me. Their one-ness was an obvious ingredient for a perfect existence. Ugliness too! I wondered. Could they have already conquered outward beauty? And what would we do if we could? I began to seriously consider this possibility. All mysteries are rooted in fact and we do have the worldwide alien phenomenon. They are "ugly" and outward beauty does give us power over one another.

Then it hit me. The fall of the Gods is about power. This has to be the reason for our ongoing separation. The power story is also universal. Religion was yielding plenty of clues that pointed to the aliens. Let's go back to my first solid piece of evidence: the "up" factor. All religions agreed. God/Gods aren't from here. They are from the Heavens/space. Their "up-ness" indicated possible flying devices. Why would spirits come from "up?" This is only logical for physical beings that conquered space/Heaven, not spirits. The Bible describes fiery chariots in the sky. There are also many ancient artworks supporting this logic. (See illustrations on front and back cover of this book.) However, they aren't chariots. Instead they look like flying saucers!

The first book investigates the Jews. They were priests who came from the Sumerians. Their depiction of God is a circle with wings. It literally describes a flying saucer. (See pictures inside.) The evidence of a religion cover-up became and is overwhelming. Therefore, I will now present my accumulation of evidence for the sake of continuity and simplicity. Now, let's go back to the beginning of my first book and this prophetic dream!

I'm having a dream and suddenly awake to the horror of being shot by a preacher. Had I been shot? Where was I? I was gripped with fear and instantly saw that I wasn't in Ohio and it wasn't 1989. The calendar on the wall read January 1, 2001. "What 2001?" I blurted out! And why had I been shot by . . . a preacher? The title of my first book was about to reveal this answer and something else. Something that hadn't happened since I was a kid! When I finally realized that I wasn't shot, I looked around. "What the . . ." I screamed again! I was naked and meditating in a motel room! Where was I and what was going on? I must be dreaming. Dreaming, hell, this is a nightmare. I needed to wake up. I needed to know what was going on.

Then I saw it. *The New York Times* newspaper was lying in my lap. I nervously picked it up.

Sweat was streaming down my face and my stomach was in knots. It was as if I already knew what it would say. I immediately got a dreadful premonition. A terrible gut feeling came over me. It haunted me for what seemed like an eternity. My hands trembled. I lifted the paper. "Oh my God," I gasped aloud. I knew it. I knew what it was going to say. "I" was about to present scientific evidence that aliens were the gods of primitive man. This is crazy. But was it?

Then I suddenly remembered. I remembered back to that horrifying moment as a child. I was only six years old. "No," I screamed! Waves of panic racked my body. I started shaking convulsively. It scared me to remember. I was so young and it was at night. My family and I were watching a comedy show, "The Red Skelton Hour." I was lying on the floor when I looked up and saw him. What started as a beautiful evening of entertainment turned into a horrible nightmare. I saw this man looking at me from outside my window. He wasn't just an ordinary man, though. He had a large bald head and huge black eyes. I remembered screaming hysterically as my family rushed to my side. They calmed me but later talked about it being a demon.

I was afraid to be alone from then on. I don't remember anything about that year. My first and second grade is a blank to this day. I am still afraid to be alone. I got angry at myself. What am I saying? I'm a grown man. I shouldn't be afraid. I shook my head and wiped away the tears. I got even angrier at myself for crying. I looked again at the headlines. "Showdown The Two Witnesses and Christianity." I couldn't believe what I was reading. It not only confirmed my premonition but completely validated my dream. I read on. I was about to go on the Antonio show and debate religion with my scientific discoveries! "Scientific discoveries of what?" I remarked dumb-founded. "I'm not a scientist!" And then I realized why I said "I." Jake wasn't here! Even though he's the other witness in these books I had the alien experience. I looked at the date.

That moment changed my life forever. That and what was about to happen next. The paper was from the future! It was tomorrow's, January 2, 2001. I dropped it and fell back against the wall. I was in shock. I covered my face in disbelief. I slowly uncovered my eyes. Then it happened! I saw three figures standing at the foot of my bed. There were two Roswell Aliens on either side of a tall thin naked man. Suddenly they disappeared.

This is what my first book is about and ultimately this one too. Could this man have been Jesus? He said that he came from "Heaven above." And last but not least, could we be them? Is he one? He said that we need to "return." The aliens say the same thing and they do come from above. Could we be them from the future? This was intriguing because I do have deja vu. I felt like I was from the future.

Time traveling to our past is theoretically possible according to science. We found a scripture about the angels that supported this possibility. It is in the New Testament, from the book of Jude, and was the focus of our search. Mine quickly turned toward the aliens. Anyway, he quotes a much older writer prophesying about angels leaving their first estate for a strange flesh. Could we be these "angels"/Aliens "which left their first estate for a strange Flesh"? This scripture is just one of many challenging the Jewish religion. It is proof of their information cover-up. This fact alone was the driving force of my alien origin theory. It is a quote by Enoch, only the seventh from Adam. His book is canonized out of the Old Testament even though it is much older than Genesis.

Could mankind be the strange flesh? Enoch makes reference to these angels as the fugitive serpent. DNA is represented by serpents. The devil is a serpent. Serpent symbols and worship are universal! Mankind is still a mystery today and our heads are too large. Could we be this strange flesh that they scientifically created with the knowledge of DNA, the serpents?

If the angels/gods are aliens, it would explain why primitive man universally called the owl the wisest bird. It is the bird that flies at night. It has a big head and eyes to match like the aliens. (See Owl Man on back cover and inside pictures.) Could this reasoning also be connected to today's alien abductions? They are similar. That's strange enough for me! All of these facts would explain deja vu, reincarnation, head-molding, and prophecy or predestination. Most of all, it would explain our unnatural addiction to outward beauty. I am addicted to beautiful women and I have deja vu!

Enoch prophesied that "the angels return to this strange flesh; like a dog returning to vomit; like a pig returning to waller in mire/mud." We are carbon-based organisms. Every living thing is mud, just like the Jewish creation story says! I started brainstorming. Maybe it isn't possible to change the future, just foretell it. My buddy experienced the Mothman and he confirmed this. He also has big eyes, moth-like wings and the body of a man. Sounds like these angels/aliens weren't completely successful in their scientific manipulation of primates. (The evidence supports this. See pictures!)

The objectives they were trying to reach are obvious. They wanted man to have unlimited sight, flight, and power! Scientific genetic abnormalities like this and the Greek Centaur are also universal. The prophets, Shamans, medicine men, and Jesus confirm prophecy as well. Prophecy is predicting the future. The aliens do, too. Science supports this reality with the grandfather paradox. Jesus does the same with his scripture about the "elect." He said it wasn't possible to deceive them. The election and its outcome is already known. We are all predestined. They were sent just like him. Sent back!

Man, what an unbelievable possibility. Would we really welcome it? Everyone would see our mistakes. I didn't like that. I would sure like to do some of it over again. Thankfully, not most, I resisted revenge!

The first book ended with my prophetic dream becoming a reality. On our journey we discovered that Jesus is a false translation. "No way!" Christianity is the world's largest religion. How could this be? Worse yet, no one seemed to care. Moreover, his true name validated my scientific evidence about our origins. If the angels/gods are the aliens then his name would validate it. I am and Yeshua! Whoa! Unbelievable, and English is the Earth's dominant language! His name isn't Jesus! He even said, "I will be hated for my name's sake" and "I came to save that which is lost." That's why I put "WWYD" in the atom's center on every book. This is unreal!

These are provable facts but would the world believe me? I can't perform any magic. Yes, it's just "me" at the end. Jake (the other witness?) doesn't agree with my findings about the aliens. He is still brain-washed by primitive man's "spirit" teaching just like the rest of the world. Or at least the majority of it. This is obviously why the prophecy involves two men. Their struggle must parallel the world's biggest challenge. Science versus Religion. Ours did.

Could I be Michael? I don't know. Is this why I chose to use my first name only on these books? I still didn't know. But I definitely knew Jake. And he didn't agree with my alien/angel theory. I didn't think that neither he nor I was worthy of being the two witnesses. This is important! But if contact is about the aliens I would be the logical candidate.

These books and the evidence speak for themselves. "Trust the evidence and not man!" This is a quote by Grissom of C.S.I. Crime Scene Investigation. Earth is the crime scene. Why else would we still be digging up our past? Think about it. Get ready to meet "The Two Witnesses"! But remember, we all make it in the end. Yeshua's quote on the back of my second book will confirm this! The outcome isn't scarier than our present reality. The future is bright! But for some of us it could be the beginning again. That's scary!

Our past is ugly. I had just begun to discover

ancient Alien evidence in the first book. I was catapulted onto the national scene with its success. My book was dangerous because it threatened the validity of religion. I had only presented three illustrations of ancient alien evidence. However, they supported my alien origin conclusion and blatantly challenged religion. At its end though, I was flabbergasted by another shocking discovery. Gold replaces Ozone layers. We have a big hole in ours! I immediately realized that the quote "Heaven's streets are paved with gold" was scientific. The universe's planets are terra-formed with gold. The gold halo became the universal holy symbol. Wow! This makes sense! The gods explore and live in space only with gold's protection!

Gold would eventually hold the key to solving our mystery. It is also universal. The gods needed it. We do too. Read on! I knew then why the gold halo became the angels'/gods' symbol. Man wouldn't have an ugly God. (See picture of Aborigine God; it connects aliens to gold and flying saucers!) This fact alone epitomized our ancient and ongoing addiction to outward beauty. Modern man became God! (See symbols for God and Babylonian man riding chariot in the circle.)

My alien answer tortured my buddy and nearly everyone else around me. They're hung up on a "spirit" existence and have no ancient evidence to support it. Heck, it isn't logical either. How do you create a spirit? How do they live? My buddy couldn't answer these questions and the world is still waiting for proof of this spirit existence. One thing's for sure: If anyone could prove it, it would make lots of money. And that alone rules it out. Believe me, just ask everybody. I think the majority would agree.

Anyway this gold evidence comes from ancient Sumerian clay tablets. They also show a tenth planet in our solar system. There are even more alien statues from Israel. These were found along the banks of the Jordan River. The world should've seen this evidence by now. What am I saying? They already have! Or have they? I didn't until I was thirty-five. But it was already made famous by author Zechariah Sitchin in 1982. How could this be and why isn't it in our science books? The solar system on the clay tablet is depicted exactly as today's science pictures it. Our satellites haven't photographed the tenth planet because it has an elliptical orbit. This takes it far into the reach of space before it returns. Then it happens, we spot it!

These tablets reflect an orbit of seven thousand years. We are ruled by the Jewish calendar of six thousand years. Think about this; come on. I even discovered a thousand-year reign of peace. It happens upon contact in the Revelation prophecy. Six plus one equals seven! This is their orbit cycle! The ancient Ankh supports its existence as well; science does, too. It is appropriately called Planet X, the Roman numeral ten. So shouldn't we ask again, "how can this be?" Why don't we know about it!

But then again the first book's title is self explanatory. We all know how governments/religions cover things up. They're one and the same. Hell, conquest has a history of destroying the enemies' historical records. That's why we mourn the lost library of Alexandria and before that the Egyptians. The world was ruled by Roman teachings for thirteen hundred years. And they thought the world was flat! When the first book ended I was still learning about gold, the tenth planet, and even more ancient alien artworks. Wow, it was going to have a sequel and it does. It is appropriately titled *Aliens Gold Tenth Planet*! But did I get killed at the end as the dream implied? I obviously didn't, but do I get shot? Is it really just a dream? Remember, my discovery that dreams foretell the future in Judaism, could be a reality! They are even the "real" world in some religions. They are sacred in all.

Was this dream the future? Did I get shot? As you read earlier I did! It is how the first book ends and the second book begins. The second book has more explosive evidence like an alien "mother goddess" statue on the front cover. This supports the "sons of god" story in Genesis of my first book. More importantly it shows us what these God's look like. The Aliens! Their story is reflected on the back cover of this book along with the giants of Easter Island. They are the product of this mixture. These sons of god looked "down" on the daughters of men and saw they were "pretty." They had sex and begat giants. How could this happen if they were spirit? This is what the book of Enoch is about. The woman's body on the mother-goddess statue is fat. In ancient times it represented beauty. The head is alien-looking. It supports my findings.

It is what these gods looked like.

We even have a religious yin/yang symbol that looks like two sperms and an egg. This is how science would achieve this. I put it above the statue's head. You can clearly see the scientific connection just like the halo and gold. It is the alien sperm/DNA and primitive man sperm/DNA! And we do have a missing link! The first book has the Shroud of Turin on the front cover. I theorize that it is the authentic burial cloth of Jesus. He left it as a sign to tell us where Heaven is, space! The shroud looks like the night sky and its many stars. Heaven is the universe/space. This is our future and where they obviously live in spaceships. They have already conquered space and omni presence! It's where science is hoping to conquer soon because religion is threatening our very existence.

The second book presents even more scientific discoveries of ancient alien evidence. It also presents my further understanding of quantum physics. Atoms make up the universe. This would explain why Jesus said, "Heaven is within us." The Bible calls man Adam. He is made of atoms. It explains why the Egyptian god is called Atum. He is the first and came from nun nothing! He creates the other nine, which makes ten like the ten planets. Coincidence? And yet they are all one. This sounds like god, the angels, and cloud "nine"! It sounds like the Greeks and their twelve gods (10 planets, sun, and moon). We have twelve houses in the zodiac and twelve months and twelve tribes of Israel. It also sounds like today's big bang theory! Atum, the Egyptian god, seeded the universe through mastur- bation! The universe is like an egg with infinite eggs within itself. Eve came from Adam!

Atoms can't be created nor destroyed and they are timeless. So how is there a beginning? At- oms have no beginning! And how was Adam creat- ed when we can't create atoms? Well, scientifical- ly of course, with mud! Our building blocks have always existed and maybe us too! This will help to solve the enigma of time itself. Read on!

Finally my story climaxes with this third and final book. It contains even more ancient evidence of aliens and flying saucers. And then it happens! I discovered an authentic photo of Johnny Cash looking at a flying saucer. Is this just a coincidence? My dream starts in Nashville. Could it end here? It is the capital of country music and Bible publishing. I had to use it.

But how could it end here? I wrote my death and resurrection in Israel, at the end of the second book. Get ready for the twist of a lifetime. Contact brings me back to Nashville where it all began. I'm about to take a ride on the clouds. Wow! Just like Jesus' second coming. Even this "second coming" prophecy supports my flying saucer reality. He's coming on the "clouds" where every eye will see. This sounds like world-wide contact by flying saucers. Also, why would spirits come on clouds and from up? We do have ancient historical artworks showing mass sightings, and it is a round world! How else could "everyone" see him at the same time? Could he and the Aliens be the gods of primitive man? Are we really seeking knowledge of the universe/Heaven? This is a logical prerequisite to be with those who are smarter than us. The evidence supports this outcome and it is logical. Are we prepared to be outwardly ugly and equal again like the giants of Easter Island? Are we seekers of scientific knowledge? If so then, are we ready to turn our backs on mankind as they do? Did Johnny? Do any of us really? I'm writing this book, aren't I? So I obviously don't.

I am addicted to beauty. I don't want to be ugly. If science provides me with a choice, I don't know what I'd do. I know what I would've done without this knowledge. But now I know the misery of mankind's gamble, especially when I look at the cross. Yet I'm still unsure of what I would do. I suddenly remembered an amazing discovery. It is the world's most famous alien abduction case of Travis Walton. He saw beautiful humans with the aliens. Could knowledge give us the best of both worlds? Is this possible as long as we can control our sexual emotions? Read on and learn more about primitive man's traditions to overcome sexual jealousy!

What will we do though if "returning" is "really" the only scientific fact that matters? What if it is the ultimate challenge once we solve our mystery? Do we all have to be Jesus? Is this the ultimate test to re-enter this beautiful utopia? "Rich men don't enter" into matters of fact. And, unfortunately we're brainwashed from the get-go to be rich! Riches are all about power, and power is all about beauty of the flesh. And it's ultimately all about sex.

Life is a real catch-22. Most people want to get rich so they can buy an island and stock it with the most beautiful sex partners possible. It is the most powerful addiction and problem plaguing mankind. (See Cernes Giant.) We do kill others for sex and we do have AIDS. And if that isn't enough proof, we even judge our moral character by it. The more you have the worse your moral character.

Remember "enter" is the key. Could the universal act of transcendental meditation or mystery be "the way"? It is universal! Science calls this biorhythm feedback. FEEDBACK! I thought again about the "pride of man song" and the lyrics "turn around go back down back where we came from"! Are we addicted to outward beauty? Does beauty rule in our society? This is the simplest evidence. Remember Occam's Razor? Children will all agree that it does. Truth comes from the mouth of babes! And I said I am!

Look at the matching symbols. They make scientific creation possible. The evidence supports aliens manipulating primates. Was it for the pursuit of power? The power story is in every culture! It is also universal. Could we be these angels addicted to this strange flesh? Does poetic justice have us fulfilling our own neverending need for gold because of this addiction? Have we become slaves and a necessary evil of the universe because we could?

We know it isn't possible to prevent or stop scientific discoveries. Many famous people, the Bible, and even science support this reality. It's time to wake up! We can't stop scientific achievement! Are we asleep or just brainwashed by religion? We've banned cloning because our president is religious but it's being done elsewhere! And what about stem cell research, would he ban it if he needed it? I think not! Could we have become beautiful humans in a universe that forbids it because we can't maintain perfection? If so, aren't we just unassuming workers for the propagation of our own species? We do need Earths! And the fact is, nobody likes hard work. Digging gold is hard work!

Do you remember my creation question earlier? Is our creation forbidden because of this obvious weakness in controlling it? The Cernes Giant supports this "ugly" fact of mankind. (See picture inside.) So do all the sex crime offenders that fill our prisons. Finally, this is the real "ugliness" of mankind that I think we can all agree on. This and death makes us blind to outward beauty. It is what makes scientists of us all.

It's painfully obvious that mankind is a scientific possibility with disastrous consequences. We are the most destructive force on this planet. Therefore we must be a controlled experiment for the good of our future! Predestination supports this reality! Ancient artworks do, too! Even religious books that "we can't trust" have this common theme. Indians don't trust man with writings. Neither do any other tribal peoples. I don't think our every move is controlled just repeating itself. Jesus is the most famous and the Jewish religion dominates the Earth! It is destined! It isn't done by magic. It would be easy to scientifically manipulate us and Yeshua is anti-religion. Science must rule if this is a controlled addiction! (See last page.) Beautiful humans, spare body parts, and artificial workers are realities of our own future? It's obvious that no artificial worker can do what fierce, competitive, evil humans can do. We compete to the point of killing each other!

Can "my" scientific scenario be proven? The

game of the Olmec gods support "my" conclusion. The mother goddess statue does as well. And remember we do have a missing link in our fossil record. It is illustrated on the evolutionary chart. (See pictures inside.) This reality explains why they don't exist with us. They obviously aren't spirit and can't stop us from killing them! If they were they wouldn't have any reason not to be here. This is logical.

Abstinence must be the only way! We have to cure ourselves. Our separation occurred after "we/angels/aliens" mixed with primitive man. How can a spirit mix with a flesh and blood being? Again, if you haven't found any ancient depictions of God or angels then you are closing your mind to other evidence. This is called being religiously brainwashed. His ancient artworks like the Mother Goddess Statue prove this cohabitation. The "giants" and man multiplied rapidly and "wickedness spread all over the Earth." We not only achieved global wickedness but even wiped out Neanderthal. The separation was caused by a flood. This is universal.

Then the mystery of modern man began with religion. This is a scientific fact. It is prevalent in every religion, and this sequence of events is proven by science! But it will take contact to solve our mystery. The prophecies of all cultures agree. I do too! Some people will never leave their traditional religion! Contact is the cure for man's religious differences. Even the "two witnesses" of the Jews are killed. But the Bible says they "have spirit power." Their deaths refutes this obvious embellishment. They have no magic spirit power! And, obviously Yeshua didn't either.

Anyway, the world rejoices because their answer is torturous. Coincidence! But "three" days later they are resurrected! Three is universally common and we are the third rock from the sun. Great song Joe! Remember, I became a famous country music star! Ha, ha. Anyway, and then Michael leads the battle to stop the kings of the Earth from destroying it. Contact is made because of man's global threat to destroy the Earth. Could the Jewish Star be proof of this inevitable event? It does match the atom and Yeshua is Jewish. He is the most famous man on Earth and "allowed" himself to be killed. He was killed because of his "peace" protest. There is other proof too that contact will happen because of a global nuclear event. (See Cernes Giant, Hopi

Prophecy, and Mars and Satellite Man on clay tablet.)

But, could we relive Yeshua's life through it? Is our ultimate sacrifice the mystery itself? Mystery is the universal act of a peaceful protest. He was teaching it. If so WWYouDo? We know "WWJD", but what would Yeshua do? George Bush represents Jesus and WWJD Christianity. Remember the evidence suggests that there isn't any blinking thinking magic. I challenge religion to prove their primitive "spirit" teaching once and for all. Otherwise we must consider the Alien evidence.

We must ban religion and chart a scientific course for the future. We must do this for the sake of our children and "The Future Alien Contact." Please look at the aborigine cave art one more time. (It's the second picture.) It is one of the oldest depictions of God. It is an alien in a flying saucer and has a Gold halo! Please, contact is just the beginning! My struggle continues. "This is my final answer! Now, look at the Cernes Giant". Remember "Who Wants to be a Millionaire"? Just apply Occam's Razor and the answer is "simple"! The answer to our mystery is too.

The Future Alien Contact

P.S. Well, read on and discover what I do with my millions. You too can win the million dollar prize mentioned in the dedication! I want to thank all of you who would do the same. I do put another warning on the back cover of my second book. It reads, "Warning: Solving this mystery may be harmful to your wealth." I dedicate these books to scientific discovery. Challenge everything, even me! Einstein is always quoted about embracing the mysterious, and I agree wholeheartedly. But I like his quote about patriotism. He said, "Patriotism is the most insidious disease of mankind. Religion is too!" He is universally revered as a genius!

P.S. Thanks Moze for your beautiful artwork!

The Future
Alien Contact

December 21 2012

Chapter 1

"It's time!" Then it happened. Resurrection, contact, and finally peace! This was the last thing I remembered before I left my body. I blacked out. Blacked out to waking up! I woke up outside my body. And just like my first and only near-death experience when the preacher shot me I was invisible and moving. Moving away from myself fast.

What, this again! Instantly I remembered that horrifying moment. Out-of-body experiences have a terrible side effect. It's called vertigo, and I dreaded the awful stomach sickness that came with it. Vertical! Wow, this is the up thing again.

"Oh no," I cried out. "It's happening again." I was moving faster and faster away from myself. At least I knew where I was going, this time. I was going home, "my first estate" as Enoch said in the book of Jude. I wasn't scared because I was pre-pared. I had finally come to terms with my outward ugliness, or at least I thought so.

"What am I saying?" I wasn't ready. Other than my encounter when I was six, the dream, and the first OBE experience I hadn't experienced open contact. I haven't been abducted that I remember anyway. I knew that I still wasn't ready personal-ly. I was, however, convinced of the alien existence, but I was still addicted to outward beauty. I was ad-dicted to the outward beauty of everything. Then I thought of the Cernes Giant. The sheer brutality of mankind brought me back to reality. It kept me in check. I had to be ready. I was convinced that our future had already happened. The evidence sup-ported it. Religion and Einstein say that time could be manipulated and really doesn't exist. We have to be ready all the time. Our past is primitive and scary!

I felt confident in overcoming my addict-ed to sexual beauty. This is what the Cernes Giant represents. But I was still a work in progress, even though I became a scientist. I was unsure of myself. However, knowledge was the most exciting thing to me now. My children and children of the world are what I love the most. This is the rock that I hold on to. Knowledge matured me, and the alien evidence changed me forever.

I am a scientist. I saw their ugliness and sameness as attributes of a perfect society. I was willing to give up the hell of mankind to help the children of the world. I saw the future in them and a cure for our own problems. Our different looks and sex don't mix.

I still thought about the most famous alien abduction ever, of Travis Walton. It defied my reasoning except for one possibility. He saw beautiful humans with the aliens. I knew that this could only be possible with knowledge and maturity. But did they have sex? Sexually jealously was our problem. The Cernes Giant made this perfectly clear. Then I realized that the tribal communities of the world force yearly orgies for this reason. Humans could perfect this weakness. They had to do it with practice, and it was the most difficult thing in their tribe to overcome. The tribe was the family.

I immediately thought of Hillary Clinton's book and how it epitomizes this conclusion. In Africa a village raises the child. Our sexual flaw is so obvious. I felt as if I could convince the world with this, my alien evidence and knowledge of predestination. Destiny is time travel. Mankind is a controlled scientific experiment that shouldn't have ever happened. But it did and we made "good" use of it.

We need gold, and nobody likes hard work to get it. I will convince the world with my aborigine cave drawing of God. It is clear that their god is an alien and has a halo around his head. Most importantly, it shows they came in flying saucers. I loved it. Omni-presence, "up-ness/flying saucers" and their need for gold is all right here for the world to see. The cave drawing is older than any book written by "modern man."

These are not only the common denominators of all religious beginnings but also the title of my second book: *Aliens Gold Tenth Planet*. My research into the origins of religion led me to these facts. I discovered that primitive man was manipulated by the aliens to make a "tiller of the ground." Hence, all religions have "creation" stories. This became the mystery of modern man, the missing link. And all this for gold! It makes ozone layers and can repair them. We have a big hole in ours now.

Man, I love this! The evidence speaks for itself. It is our past. Suddenly I realized that I must have convinced the world with my books. What am I saying? It even became a movie. I had to. I'm here in Israel, and it's 2012. My Mom is in a strange suit saying that Jerusalem had been nuked. We were in a makeshift hospital and I was lying on a gurney when I woke up.

Woke up, hell! I must be resurrecting now or resurfacing! Wow. This is unbelievable. I tried to remember back to 2003 but I couldn't remember past the first book signing of my second book in 2003. I was scared and desperately wanted to remember. My life flashed before my eyes in an instant. I not only wrote a second book but even wrote a third. Man, I couldn't believe what was happening. The past eight or nine years started playing in my head like a movie on fast forward. What! I even wrote a third book called *The Future Alien Contact*. What did it say? Did I foretell the future correctly in my books? I couldn't remember a thing.

Suddenly I realized that I was in the tunnel

again. Would I see my dad again like I did the first time? I didn't. I was hurtling toward the light at a tremendous speed. "The light, oh no!" I knew it was me; I was about to enter my body again. Oddly enough, I wasn't scared. I even wondered for just a moment if this tunnel was an e-string in space. I thought about our fiber optics reality and digital information. Could memory be part of a cosmic digital universe?

I was still invisible to myself. And for a split second I thought about the remote viewing possibility. I tried it. I saw Mom, Nurse Gail, and Jake in my head like I was there. I had sat up and was doing mystery. Cameramen were trying to talk to me while Mom and Nurse Gail were acting confused. They were comforting each other and trying to figure out what to do. They wanted the cameramen to leave us alone and were beginning to cry.

I wanted to help. I was powerless. All I could do is watch until it happened. But I didn't watch long. I opened my eyes; I was an alien! I took a good look at myself. I was sitting in a lone seat with a control device to my right. Wow, I was actually in a spaceship. I laughed because I always thought the right-hand seat of God sounded like a pilot and co-pilot. Then I saw them. I saw the same man in my dream with two aliens on either side. They looked just like me!

"Welcome home," he said softly. I didn't respond. I was still in shock. Where was Jake, I wondered? Is he one of the aliens beside this man, who must be Yeshua? Was I Michael the arch-angel? Why wasn't he here? I had so many questions running through my mind. I laughed again at the arch-angel's title. It sounded like a ship's captain.

"You will know soon enough," he assured me, stepping even closer. The aliens advanced at the same time. They were standing within arm's reach of me.

I tried hard to remember the last eight or nine years. Hell, I couldn't remember past the moment we went to war with Iraq. "Went to war!"

"No," I screamed out! Suddenly, I remembered. Was my nephew alive? Waves of fear swept through my body again. Only this time it was like the pain of possibly losing your own child. All of my nieces and nephews were like my own children. Hell, what am I talking about? I love all children. I needed to know if this happened, and I had to know now. I had to know if Danny was alive.

"Is my nephew alive?" I cried out uncontrollably. They were all looking me right in the eyes but didn't show any emotion. I couldn't read an answer in their expressions.

"Please," I begged. "I've got to know."

They again just stared back at me. I started to wonder if I were one of them or not. I looked down at myself. Yes, I was an alien, and it didn't surprise me. I remember I had just looked at myself and the man before me had also just spoken to me. He welcomed me "HOME."

Man! This is unbelievable. My mind started racing, and the memories began to flood back. I remembered back to the limo in 2003. We had just heard about the war, and I must've passed out. My nephew was in the Marines. I couldn't remember anything after that. I didn't want to. Yet!

I quickly asked the man if my nephew was alive. "Yes, your nephew is alive. Now please calm yourself as we have much work to do."

"We?" I asked weakly.

"Yes, we," and then he reached for my control module. There was a tubular device with an hour-glass shape and a handprint at the top beside my seat. I suddenly thought about my thumbprint and using it on the first book. I proposed that mine matched the orbit of the tenth planet. It was elliptical shaped like the Ankh. And since they are unique it would validate my role as the alien representative. Would it?

He turned the control toward himself. He looked at me and said, "Don't be afraid." Then he lay his hand in it.

"Oh my god," I gasped in complete shock as the ship suddenly disappeared. This same thing happened to Travis Walton. I looked around and saw so many other saucers that I couldn't begin to number them. They reached as far as the eye could see. I looked back at this man. He must be Yeshua, I thought to myself.

"Yes, I am,'" he said calmly.

His response rattled me. But I immediately calmed down and figured as much. He comforted me telepathically. Hell, I laughed to myself, he was "O.K."! After all, "Jesus" could read minds. I wondered suddenly if he knew I just said his name in my mind. He smiled and I knew he did. I wasn't afraid, just a little scared. I mean, for God's sake, I was in open space. I started to ask him about his magic-like abilities and such but he started explaining before I could ask.

"What you want to know you already know," he said softly. It was so quiet that you could here a pin drop. "And yes, you are in a spaceship."

I knew that I had to be. There wasn't any coldness, wind, or anything. It was as if I were a hologram. I reached to touch myself.

"Yes, you are real," he remarked simultaneously as I did. He took his hand out of the control and the ship instantly appeared. He turned it toward me. I didn't ask anything this time. He told me telepathically. He wanted me to do this. He also continued to tell me there isn't any thing called spirit magic. It's called science. He suddenly spoke.

"I am not greater than my father," he said as he looked to his left and right. "And he isn't any greater than me. We are one." He was confirming everything my research concluded. We are the aliens and are the fathers of mankind. The fathers of time and ourselves. Mankind is the mother. Wow, this sounded like Eve's creation from Adam's rib! He was even put in a deep sleep. It was scientific surgery! We are male and female. We created her by mixing our DNA and primates (primitive man). We created the mystery of modern man. And then we became it, through downloading memory into her. We continue through her/mankind's body addicted to our beautiful worker. It gives us birth/death again and again until we resurrect through the mystery.

The mound Indians of southern Ohio taught that we are trapped in this body and must project our spirit back to the Heavens upward. There's that vertical thing again. They do the mystery to be born again of the spirit. It is universal.

I had lots of questions, but I knew this was a fact. And Yeshua knew it. I went ahead and put my hand in the control. The ship disappeared. I don't know why but I laughed openly. This was just amazingly too cool. I lifted my hand and it reappeared. I laughed out loud again and couldn't stop myself from talking.

"Man, this is cool, Yeshua."

"Yes, it is," he replied with a hint of excitement to his voice. This took me by surprise. It was his first sign of emotion and our first bit of casual dialogue.

"Yes," he continued equally as casual. "I am also constantly impressed by the wonder of the universe myself. Heaven is truly a spectacular thing. You could even say it's more precious than a newborn baby."

I looked at him in complete astonishment. To me nothing was more precious than a newborn baby. He immediately remarked that the universe gives life to newborns, this ship, everything, and they are one and the same. So it is more fragile than even the baby itself. Now, I understood. Serving the universe is the most important part we can play. Without the "whole" universe our "part" wouldn't exist. I understood but I wondered about the possibility of being other living things. It is taught. I wanted to understand this oneness principle of life more but before I got a chance to ask he gave me my answer. It was the principle of quantum physics.

Our every thought and action is reflected on the universe itself. The animals, birds, fish don't worry. Babies don't think, only adults who teach that life is a right or wrong issue. I told them to just be good to each other. And it was time to control my thinking for the good of the universe. Again I suddenly realized that the aliens weren't talking. He responded before I could ask.

"They are the way. They don't have to talk. They read each other's minds."

Wow, I thought to myself. No wonder they don't have any problems. And then I laughed to myself. No wonder their heads are so big, too. I was still looking at Yeshua.

"Don't worry," he said cool like. "I know what you mean. I know that you really don't have any judgment toward outward ugliness. You've at least overcome that, but you haven't overcome the real evil of the universe. It is your sexual addiction to outward beauty. You just haven't remembered your pain in awhile though. Now it's time to remember. Are you ready?"

I went from being completely at ease to being afraid again. I just wasn't ready. I knew that I had to have done terribly wrong to be a human again. I had made some terrible mistakes. I threw myself at his feet and begged for his and everybody's forgiveness. I cried and cried repeatedly saying that I had done wrong. "I am so so sorry."

He pulled me to my feet and lifted up my chin level with his own. "Because you know we are evil you will overcome this evil. Mankind is the evil of the universe! You have sought the kingdom of Heaven and it stands before you now." I looked at him and he looked back with a stare that said everything. It wasn't telepathic either. It was something that I already knew.

"Yes," he said looking to his right. "This is me," and then he looked to his left. "And this is your friend Jake. We must sacrifice ourselves through the mystery. You used to do this. I understand why you almost stopped."

"But…" I started to talk. He interrupted me.

"I know that you tried. I know your life," he reassured me lovingly. "And in a moment you will remember it, too. I want you to and you want to. You sought so hard to find it and I know that you tried. In fact, you found the answer. You sought the mystery to the kingdom of heaven. You do mystery!

Now I want you to prepare yourself for the truth. It is a hard thing for mankind. But it is truly a beautiful reward for us all. For it is a life without pain, sorrow, and death. It is the way."

He took the alien on his right by the hand and proceeded to sit down. They sat facing each other and started doing the mystery. I knew what they were doing. To know the mystery, we must do the mystery. It sounds easy but very few find it, let alone do it. It's the only way to control our mind. And life is all mind over matter. Then, I suddenly realized he might sacrifice his human form through human combustion.

I wanted to ask him about Jake. As I thought about this, the alien standing before me said he was Jake. It really shocked me. I couldn't believe what I was hearing. But I couldn't stop wondering about spontaneous combustion. I had written about it in my first book. Was Yeshua going to make his human form combust? Is this how it happens?

We do have evidence of spontaneous human combustion. Was he literally going to sacrifice his human form like his parable suggests: "A tree can't yield fruit unless its seed dies and falls to the ground." Do we have to sacrifice ourselves by doing mystery until we die? (Little did I know I finally provided this evidence. See pictures.)

I wondered about this. I had always struggled with it ever since my research led me to Yeshua and the mystery. But I didn't get to wonder long.

The Alien startled me again by responding. "Yes we must break this addiction, and the mystery is the way. You almost gave up on it."

He was right, I had. It tortured me. Everything I had done wrong also tortured me. I felt like this was our best proof of time travel. Our conscience! Why else would we have it? We're the only thing that commits suicide. I knew this. I missed my brother so bad. He did it. But I thought about Yeshua's quote on the back cover of my second book: "Many are first that shall be last and last that shall be first." This fact always comforted me. We will all be back together again. The Alien immediately agreed. What do I mean, the alien was Jake?

He continued, "You were right. We can scientifically create another human. It's going on as we speak. It is the struggle of the universe, an awful creation. And yet it has become its own necessary evil. We cannot stop this creation and desire for outward power. It is everywhere and infinite like us and the universe. They are doing this all the time. This is why they crashed in Roswell. They also make mistakes in their pursuit of power. But mankind is not a good creation. It is not nature's creation. You know this."

Wow, I did, or at least it's what I had concluded from the evidence. This is what my research kept pointing to, but what about Travis Walton? What about the beautiful Humans? Could we have both? And what about Jake? The last memory that I had of him was our split over "my" alien thing. He really believed in a spirit existence. I had "angrily" told him that he was just as brainwashed as the rest of this religious world. He always laughed and said they were, but he wasn't.

I laughed then and reminded him of my Jeff Foxworthy religious redneck joke. If you think someone can be religiously brainwashed but you can't be then you could be religiously brainwashed. Then I ask them if they're religious and if they answer, "Yep, you bet," I'd tell them they could be a religious redneck. They usually didn't get it. Actually, they didn't want to get it. After I laugh and they get angry I'd have to tell them why I laughed.

Then they say, "I ain't religious I have a relationship."

"Yes," I always told them, "with a religious person."

Then they start to argue that "Jesus" ain't religious. Boy, you can't win. I couldn't win with Jake, either. I didn't want to. Facts are facts. "Jesus" is the biggest religion on Earth. It is religion! Oh well, I had so many questions. He knew it too and began to reassure me about Jake. Aha, they still aren't in agreement if he's Jake. I knew it! We are aliens addicted to mankind's power through beauty of the flesh! We had to seek knowledge and the mystery. Mind over matter could only be achieved through the mystery. I knew that practice makes perfect.

"Your friend is all right," he said, interrupting my thought. "I'm him and he is ready. He's getting old. However he is still addicted to outward beauty, like you. And you've made your alien evidence clear. But, seeing is believing, and he will believe you this time. Anyway, you are addicted to beauty too. I know you controlled yours. You know how. Jake closed his eyes to it. His eyes won out. Knowledge is the ultimate Power. He found the mystery, you found both. The two essential things for peace."

He held up the peace sign. "It and our love for others are one and the same. Knowledge is our service and love is the sacrifice. And yes, this is the mystery. It is all about mind over matter. We all know this. But we can create. And some of us became victims of desire, thinking we could improve upon our looks. Yes, we, Michael. But the universe gave us our oneness and ability to achieve immortality. Actually, life is what it is. Nature exists the same everywhere. We knew this when we discovered this through the knowledge of science. But we wanted to be greater than one another! Science gave us this too. Outward looks became our downfall. We are the one-third angel story."

Wow! I couldn't believe my ears. I was hearing an alien tell me this for the first time. And it was Jake! This was great, because we had started there. It was what my first book, *The Two Witnesses and the Religion Cover-up*, was all about.

Jake (the alien) butted in; I couldn't help from laughing to myself. He always did. "But the Cernes Giant is the deadly result of our addiction. This disease is not new. We discovered it everywhere we went, and it happens on every inhabitable planet."

I thought about Mars. He affirmed it. Then he went on. "Our cure for this unnatural creation of mankind was time itself. And yes time is real when you're in it. We know this. That's the point of remembering what we are. We are nature's creation and conquered time because we could. But we created this."

He pointed toward Yeshua's human form. "And they created time. But they don't have to exist. We choose too. This is our mystery. Mine, yours, and the one-third. Mankind is the mystery we must solve. We are them. The animals, birds, bees, and every other living thing doesn't make time an issue. They don't create. They just exist. And they do this without malice, mind you. Of course, they kill. They survive just like the universe/Heaven itself. But they do this without premeditation. They don't judge. They don't doubt their existence. They only exist again and again. And yes, they are also killed without intent. There is no pleasure involved. This is nature. It is not perfect. And yet we have a perfect existence. We create it and maintain this through space travel," he said.

"We have no pain, death, nor misery but we can experience these things. It is natural and yet we have conquered it. We created this ability and yet nature created us. We did it by studying nature itself. The universe is creating its own existence. But not through magic, just natural selection. It's nature and it selected us. We saw the complexity of its 'seemingly' organized structure and realized that without intent, it exists in perfect harmony. And it does this without our help," he said.

"We help create Earths. It is our job. We are its children. One system feeding on another, but all connected. It created us and we created our own perfect existence. It is space. We stay away from the gravity of a black hole and flying debris. We control our destiny in space. This way we aren't killers and the killed. The universe exists and nothing threatens its existence. For this reason it is said that 'Heaven is our throne and the Earth is our footstool.' It is riddled with flying debris, the very thing you call paradise. And it is paradise! And yet we cannot control our own emotions long enough to stop its inevitable destruction. Therefore we come when we have to. That time is now. The Earth is being threatened with global nuclear war. This is predestined. It has happened before and will happen again. Our salvation is not for us, but for the good of our family. You and I are still addicted to the outward beauty of mankind. However we need Earths. The ability to sacrifice oneself for the good of the 'whole/family' is what life is all about. Individually, we are just an insignificant minuscule piece of an infinite fragile universe. And it is one world, not separate to us only mankind. He would like to think there arc parallel worlds or dimensions as science prefers. But it is one! We hide from you with technology. It's really a simple thing being invisible to the naked eye. If you spin fast enough you literally become invisible like a spinning top blurs. But man is primitive. The majority doesn't seek knowledge. Are we 'willing' to give our life for our children?" he asked.

"This is our ultimate challenge. Do we really believe in the endless possibilities of life itself? We know that life will continue to exist because it exists now! Isn't this a safe bet? Isn't that logical?"

He was looking me right in the eyes with a stare that completely drained my every thought. I'd seen that stare before. He was Jake!

"Yes, I am Jake," he said, "but I won't be doing the talking when we make contact. You have the knowledge and the evidence. You are ready to sacrifice yourself. I am still brainwashed. I have work to do."

I knew what he meant. I knew that I had written these books and reconciled our differences. I was the one who had presented this alien evidence to the world. It was all "mine."

Suddenly Jake turned and sat down on the floor beside Yeshua. I started to follow but Jake stopped me. He pointed toward the control. I knew what I had to do. I had always wanted to fly. I even dreamed that I had. Was it just a dream, though? It was so real that I wrote a song about it. But I had to do something else first. I had to do mystery! I needed to remember what had happened, since we went to war and my last book-signing in 2003. Hell, I couldn't believe I had written a third book! What was it about? I was about to find out!

I put my hand back in the control. The room became brilliantly white. Yeshua and the human disappeared. I knew where they went. He was preparing another planet for the recycling of man. Was it Mars? It seemed logical because of it being the next planet in our atmosphere to be Earth like. It was close now. We think it already was. The evidence supports it! (See Mars clay tablet picture.) There was much work to be done. There was always much work to be done. It was time. I closed my eyes.

The memories flooded back. I woke up and was lying in my mother's lap. I was in the limo. It had to be 2003. She was stroking my hair and trying to calm me down. "Please tell me Danny is alive," I cried out. "Please," I begged her.

"Michael honey, he hasn't gone to war yet, it just started."

"Oh, thank God," I replied. It felt as if the weight of the world lifted from my chest. I sat up and breathed a deep sigh of relief. Would they believe my dream? Or was it a dream? If it was, then it could be the future about to happen. I was suddenly filled with dreadful waves of fear and anxiety. I could hardly wait for it to come true, but was scared at the same time. Maybe it wouldn't. Deep down I knew that it would.

"Would you please turn the radio back on?" I quickly asked. I had immediately noticed that it was turned off. "Mike, it'll just upset you," Mom remarked with a haunting tone to her voice. Did she know?

"I can't help it. I've got to know what's going on in the war," I said.

"Mike," she pleaded, "please leave it off." She was trying desperately to stop the inevitable.

"Please, Nurse Gail? I've got to know what is going on." What am I saying? I thought to myself, I know that Danny doesn't get killed. I just dreamed it. It had to be a dream. I hope it isn't. I hope it's real. My evidence makes it possible. I'm counting on it. I pictured little Dan the man. That's what I always called him since he was little. I got overwhelmed with emotion. I loved my kids, so much. Hell, all kids.

Tears welled up in my eyes again as I looked

out the window. I didn't want to worry Mom anymore. We had cried enough. It was time to be cheerful. That's what she is, a born optimist, and that's what I'll be.

People were throwing things at the car as we passed them on the street. Man, did they ever hate my alien evidence. I couldn't believe it and they were supposed to be religious. I felt Mom hug me as I watched their hatred toward me.

"Don't worry," she said reassuringly. "They all don't hate you, see." She pointed toward a group of supporters. They were sitting in a circle with a huge peace sign in the middle. It was beautiful. I turned and hugged Mom. Nurse Gail started honking wildly. I looked at her and she was laughing and crying at the same time. She slowed the car and rolled the window down as she passed.

"Thank you," she screamed out. "We love you."

We all laughed and cried. We all held up the peace sign at the same time and said one last thing. We hollered out, "Love even those who hate you and forgive them, for they know what they do."

"Please," I cried out one more time as Nurse

Gail was forced to raise the window back up and drive on. Wow, I thought to myself. We all said it at the same time.

I leaned back into the seat and felt such a huge wave of relief come over me. Luckily, there were other people who saw mankind as a flawed creation. They did exist even though they were few and far in-between. But I knew this already from Yeshua's comment that few will enter the Kingdom of Heaven. Its real alien existence. Very few, I thought to myself as I looked at the many billboards displaying the ruler of this world. It was beautiful humans. They are the prince of the air. They make their Heaven, hell!

Hell, I loved beauty myself. But I tried to overcome the sexual jealousy from "ownership." Marriage didn't exist with the angels. That's the way it had to be. Sexual jealousy kills! Just look at the Cernes Giant. I wanted to tell the world about my discoveries. I wanted more than anything to paint a picture of their perfect existence. The Easter Island natives already have, where they all look the same and it ain't about prettiness. I know pretty is relative, but the billboards spelled out the outward prettiness. It ruled!

I was pretty famous in the United States but still hadn't seen any international fame. I just wrote that in my first book. I knew the alien-looking mother-goddess statue would do this for me as well. I wrote this in my second book. But it didn't. Little did I know, it would take a huge discovery, I made in the third book. Wow! I just dreamed the future and I wrote a third and final book. I couldn't help but wonder about the new discoveries I would find. New knowledge was so exciting to me, just like new sexual conquest used to be. But now I controlled that. I wanted the prettiest not the most. I may have gotten over mankind's number game but I was still addicted to beauty. Money could buy that! We all lose our looks. So knowledge is everything. No, love is greater. It can overcome sexual weakness. It had too! Together everything is possible!

I marveled at the idea of new discoveries— I was still mesmerized by the mother-goddess statue and its existence. Primitive man gave us statues of religion's union between the gods or angels and the "pretty" daughters of man. It is also a universal theme like gold, time, oneness, and the fall. It is the fall. This fall is what our mystery is all about, and we don't get to see the angel writings. It is the religion cover-up and my first book's focus.

I picked up my second book and looked at the obvious alien-looking head and the fat woman's body. This represented beauty to them. Not to me and our world now, I thought as I looked at the billboards. But man, times have changed and I'm glad. I guess they knew how fragile their existence was even then. They made statues to the gods who gave them knowledge and the women who gave them birth. Why don't we know how fragile our existence is?

Of course I knew why. We are consumed with sexual power. We hardly think of anything else. I looked at the statue and remembered back to the beginning of our search. This is what our search was all about. Where is Yeshua and the angels? Jake really had me believing in a spirit existence. I laughed at this now. Why would spirits be afraid to show up? And aren't we made in their image? It's so obvious that they are flesh-and-blood beings just like it says they are. Every religion stated this. How did this get turned around to be the opposite of the beginning? The whole world now believes in a spirit existence and dimensions. I couldn't stand it. It's one universe and future technologies exist now! They just stay away from us.

Then I knew how. The kings made a logical excuse for their absence. And to ignorant people magic is logical. Hell, it still is today even though science rules our schools. But does it really? I suddenly remembered how my son's teacher had told him the aliens don't exist. She did this harshly and followed with her religious belief: "only god and the angels exist." I asked my son if he asked her why they don't show. He answered: no, because he was afraid. I was upset at this. She violated his civil rights! But I wake up to the president saying we are a blessed nation, too. This is the reality of our ignorance today. It is the same as yesterday and thousands of years before it. What am I saying. Mankind is infinite, 666. What "isn't," was and will be again. We're always kept on Earth's inseperate.

Now, thankfully, we have archaeological evidence to answer why they don't show. They must be afraid, too. Why else would they stay away if they truly love us? This is a joke and we even have to beg them for a miracle. The writings say they are flesh and blood. Besides, how do they exist and how could they have sex with us? How do you create something that is immortal and doesn't have a body? As a matter of fact it's invisible/spirit (see J.W. evidence). This is ridiculous. Creating immortality is an oxymoron. Worse yet, our religious president isn't getting it. There isn't any evidence on behalf of a spirit existence then or now. And we are still gripped in this magic "spirit" teaching by primitive man.

The cold hard fact though, is that we have mother-"GODDESS" statues. They are older than any books, and they support a flesh, alien/God existence. Come on! When are we going to wake up? Hell, why would a spirit not show up? We can't hurt them! Besides, they love us don't they? This, their spirit teaching, and our creation resulting from love sickened me. (See Jehovah's Witness exhibit.) This was about power, and "the fall" makes that perfectly clear. This statue and the billboards make something else "perfectly" clear. It's all about beauty of the flesh.

Hell, I knew that and all my "friends" did

too. I wondered about Jake. Where was he? Had he stayed in Ohio all this time? My book should tell me what happened. I started to read the ending of my second book. The part called the future, the "third" chapter. I thought once more about religion's perfect magic god story. He foresaw all the hell and misery of his "perfect" creation and yet did it anyway. Come on! He didn't have to do it, and he could've done it perfectly. He created our hell! What a sick "magic Father," and he even wants worshipped. That's sick! We expect more from ourselves than we do from our heavenly father. He is a "perfectionist", though. Think about it.

I gagged at this point. The world is ruled by this kind of thinking. My body heaved and I thought I would get sick. I rolled down the window and got some air. As I was getting some air I noticed a billboard that previewed a new movie called *Bruce Almighty*. It was about Jim Carrey getting angry at god. He challenged god to give him his "power" because he thought could do a better job. He was miserable like most of mankind and really thought he could do better. Man, I couldn't believe it. It epitomized my point exactly. "Couldn't we all do a better job with "'magic powers'?" I said out loud.

"What?" my mom asked.

I repeated the question and even pointed to the billboard. They both looked at it. "Well, couldn't we?" I asked again. "I mean 'he' can do anything 'he' wants, right?" They both agreed. They were women. They got my point. I couldn't believe all women aren't offended by God being a man. I did the quote thing on women. It worked. They were finally seeing the ridiculousness of their magic perfect god. They really got it after they saw how these loving religious people wanted to kill me. It did it for them what it did it for me a long time ago.

It happened when I was a kid. First "he" picked favorites with his chosen race, the Jews. I came from a large family and I wasn't a Jew. This was wrong! Secondly, I couldn't stomach their killing god! I could easily see how it created our universal disease: Religious killing! I was shocked everytime I asked religious people how they could accept this. It's barbaric, illogical, and certainly not loving! They always said "god had to kill his children when they disobey." What!

"But would you?" I always asked them.

"Of course not!" They would always respond. "I'm not God!"

But they still didn't get it. And when they did, most tried to say god didn't kill his children. I always reminded them of the Red Sea and the Egyptians, not to mention Sodom and Gomorrah. Then I reminded them of "Jesus." He sacrificed his only "begotten" son, which sounds like the alien abduction phenomenon. (See star child skull.) Hell, man wasn't even "good" enough for this conception. Come on, I would tell them. It's time to wake up. What kind of father would do all this? If Jesus called these Jewish preachers who gave us this "holy" Bible blind, then aren't you the blind following the blind? Besides, your God tells us not to kill but does it himself. Come on! Don't we all criticize parents who are the "do as I say and not as I do" kind? Besides, he didn't kill Adam and Eve, why the Egyptians? Why his "only" son and aren't we all "his" children, too?

I would bombard them with one question after another. Most wanted to kill me; the rest just felt sorry for me. Their last statement was "I hope you find the 'truth' one day." Their truth! Yeah, sick, cruel, killing religious people "killed" me. They attack viciously. I watched them do it to Andy Rooney and daily in the newspaper editorial. Hell, the news too. They were all religiously blind following the religiously blind. We continued talking about the possibility of having "god's magic power." I laid the book down and asked them what they would do if they had it. They both said they would make the world perfect if they could.

They finally got it. But it was easy for them. One was my mother and the other was a nurse. It wasn't so easy for the rest of the adult world. I would soon read articles everywhere about this question and the movie. Children unequivocally said they would make the world perfect if they could. Science would do the same! Religious adults compromised. They said it would spoil children and make a boring world if everyone was perfect. I wonder if they ever realized heaven is perfect. They must be power drunk in entertainment. And forgot what it was like to be a kid in this cruel-ass world. I couldn't stand their answer, but I loved them. I had to. This was the hardest thing I've ever done and still do! I told them how I appreciated their answer. Mom had come a long way since the first book. She had given me the religious answer and my subsequent questioning embarrassed her. I didn't mean to. I'm sure she's had a lot of time to think about it. A lot has happened since then. Her "little boy" was shot by a preacher and predicted it!

I started reading the ending of the alien book. I wrote about Jake not being around for the last nine years, but had he? I couldn't remember. I finally started remembering the last pages of the ending. I remembered the first signing of the second book and how people hated me. Hell, it was now! I looked out the window again. They hate me so much. I remembered Billy Graham and his refusal to acknowledge Jesus' real name. I told everyone it was Yeshua and that it was changed to Zeus. They started throwing things and screaming at me: I remembered that vividly. They were the ones who said that his name is the most important and the only one that will save you, but didn't care about it. The Jews knew the importance of his name. They cared, but didn't have anyone named after him. They compromised, too, and called him Jesus. Yeshua did say they were blind.

I thought about the irony of religion and its self-righteousness. It contradicted itself. It is an oxymoron. Its very foundation is about making us be "good." This is judgmental in and of itself, but we aren't supposed to judge. It also speaks volumes about our "creation." We're inherently screwed up, flawed from the get-go. I laughed to myself. I thought of Kurt Cobain, the lead singer from the band Nirvana, who committed suicide. This isn't funny, but what a paradox, huh? Suicide and Nirvana don't go together. But then again, maybe they do. Especially in this world of mankind where you hate us, want to reach it, but your job is about us. What am I saying. Nirvana is living suicide. "I die daily." Monks commit it everyday. I did when I do mystery. I wonder if Kurt had done mystery.

He wrote this overwhelming simple phrase endlessly: "You read you judge and this sucks!" He captured religion's catch-22 perfectly. They're most famous for "Teen Spirit." This is all about sex and power, and we know it! It's a shame that we make sex so holy, but only if we're married. Then it's called love-making. No wonder they don't have marriage in heaven.

What's even worse is that we make the sexual act so dirty. It's all so twisted by religion. In fact the act is the dirtiest word there is and yet it brings forth the "glory" of us. What a paradox huh! And their god says we're good. This is such a cruel joke! Yeshua says we're evil. He says "only the angels in heaven are perfect and we 'must be perfect' to join them." I couldn't agree more and I don't like the word *agree*. Therefore, I must say, the evidence supports this reality about us. Don't believe me, Yeshua, or any man. Look at the overwhelming evidence. We are the most destructive, cruel being in the Universe! Even worse, we create our own destruction! Hell, just ask a child if we are dangerous. It is why we tell them not to talk to strangers. We are the strangers just like it says in Jude, "the strange flesh." We're all strangers!

I thought about our AIDS dilemma and this teen spirit. They are the fastest-growing segment of this fatal disease. The religion stronghold had to be broken. I knew the cure. I was reading it. I was about to read the last page and knew it was the only cure: CONTACT! I turned the final page and was floored! I'm going to write a third book. But, it was called *The Future*. It was called *The Future Alien Contact* in my dream. I laughed openly. Mom asked me what I was laughing about. I didn't answer.

My mind was racing wildly. I had made this same huge mistake in the first book. Even worse, though, I didn't plan the sequel and never made any mention of it at all. No wonder I made a mistake on this one, too. I must've been finding things right to the very end like I did with the mother-goddess statue. I used it for the cover. However, it didn't take a rocket scientist to figure out what the second book would be. I revealed what religion was covering up in the first book: *Aliens Gold Tenth Planet*. Then it hit me; I dreamed the final book's title! It wasn't what I had written in the second book, though. It really is all about CONTACT! But, it's the aliens that make man finally believe. They aren't going to show up, until they have to save us from global nuclear war. I knew that Jerusalem was the religious jewel. The bombing of it would trigger this final event.

Suddenly I realized that I dreamed this, too. That's what I wrote in the second book. It is what my dream was really all about. But this one made it clear. It does happen, and Alien Contact is our only cure. And it doesn't cure us; it just saves another Earth for a little while longer. Man gets recycled! I knew the dream was real! I had seen a Russian general saying that flying saucers had immobilized five nuclear silos. He retired shortly thereafter. The Jewish star is the atom. The evidence was clear. It was nuclear.

I had to get on my third and final book. I had to show the world my evidence, but I knew it wouldn't matter anyway. The cure is contact and I can't make them show. This is pre-destined to happen. I was going to continue to encounter the wrath of "God." Hell, I had already been shot. How much worse can it get? Why am I asking that—I do get killed! I thought about Jake. Was he one of the two witnesses; hell, was I? What am I thinking? The dream says we are. We do the mystery! We had to be. It didn't make us special, though. Maybe that's why I'm the spokesperson. I knew that we are all flawed/evil. Jake still has an ego problem. I was always his student. I laughed openly again.

"What are you laughing about?" she asked again. Curiosity was killing her.

"Oh, nothing really. I was just thinking about Jake and his spirit thinking. If we are the two witnesses I hope we never get on a talk show together. He knows it all and he's just like them. Well, at least with his spirit world anyway."

I pointed at the last group of religious haters as we pulled onto the entrance ramp of the freeway. "They really believe in a spirit world, devil and all, but can't give us proof of their existence." I laughed but with disgust. "And they hate my logic about it."

I couldn't tell her what I was really thinking, about the dream and all. I didn't know if she would believe it anyway. But I did! According to it we are the two witnesses and I am Michael the archangel. I didn't like this title. I thought we were all equal. And I know me and Jake ain't special. Hell, I even think we could be the two witnesses because we are admittedly unworthy of it. But I have to be the spokesperson for the Aliens. That's what Michael does. He "reveals" the angel. The evidence says they're aliens. Jake is definitely spirit brainwashed and religiously brainwashed. He thinks he's right. The evidence makes it perfectly clear. They are the gods of primitive man!

She laughed and shook her head in disbelief. "It is a weird coincidence, huh? You and Jake don't agree about the alien thing and he is spirit-minded like the rest of the world. Your disagreement mirrors the world's."

"Yeah, it's a coincidence all right. The world is 'full' of weird coincidences." I gave her the old quote gesture on the word *full*. While I did it. I told her it wasn't a coincidence that two witnesses solve our mystery. "It takes two to disagree." I looked at both peace/quote signs. I laughed again and said, "If you know what I mean."

She just gave me that weird look and kind of giggled. She knew and remembered her same ex-disease. I looked at nurse Gail in the mirror. She was looking at me, too. It was the same stare that I saw her give the doctors. It was no coincidence, and she was no coincidence! I suddenly inverted my two piece signs and made an "M" by joining them. This became my symbol. One name, one initial, Michael. We weren't a coincidence. I looked away and started watching the road. This wasn't the way home. I looked back into the mirror and didn't have to say a word. Nurse Gail was looking right at me. She was smiling. I thought we were on our way home, but of course we weren't. We were meeting Angel and the boys for dinner.

I laughed again. She laughed too. Mom joined in. She also knew. Wow! This was so cool, I thought to myself as we sped down the Interstate. With all this psychic stuff happening I wondered if they knew about my dream. If they did, they didn't talk about it. I did ask them about the third book. Had I started on it already?

They said that I didn't. Man, was I ever excited. I couldn't wait to find more evidence. I thought I had found the biggest thing already with the Mother-goddess statue but I hadn't. The second book isn't what propelled me to worldwide fame. I wasn't there yet. It would be something much bigger than this statue. I was about to find a picture of Johnny Cash looking at a flying saucer.

What? No way! Yes way! But how could this be? It was taken by another famous country music star whom I won't name. Little did I know that this situation would mirror my current dilemma. They are all religious, and I knew the picture–

taker. When I would ask him to use the picture he would say it is a hub-cap. He also said it was a joke on Johnny. However, it was done in open skies. How? But I would find another picture taken twenty years before to corroborate that it is indeed a flying saucer. It's a perfect match! I also tried to duplicate this event. I couldn't. I felt he was protecting his religious belief. I wasn't mad or offended. I hope I don't offend him if it's real. I'm just doing this for the evidence. I will forever apologize if I'm wrong.

I also knew this was the reason my dream changed the book title from *The Future* to add contact. It was just one of many coincidences too weird to be a coincidence, like this picture itself. I didn't have it when I finished the second book! Hell I didn't have it now, but I soon would. I wouldn't want to offend the picture taker, but I would use it. I would allege it is real. And yet I knew it would take contact to convince most religious people. The dream validated it. The picture was contact.

I didn't worry about offending religious people. They are the most resistant to believe new discoveries, new possibilities. Hell, they didn't believe in anything they couldn't see. Funny, huh? They really lived by the non-religious "seeing is believing" creed. But it really isn't funny, though. Most of them challenged me to make one show since I couldn't do magic. They didn't realize they couldn't make an angel or god show either. So it really didn't prove anything. But at least I looked for them! They just believed the "Holy Bible" and didn't care if it said they were flesh and blood either. I told them this is what the Pharisees and the Sadducees wanted from Yeshua. They wanted magic or to make the angels appear.

What's even sadder is my friend Jake. He didn't believe me either when I asked him if I could be Michael the Archangel. He's religious, though. He believes in the spirit world. The same thing applied to the picture-taker. He's my wife's family, and I would never ask him. I won't, either. I won't ask anyone else. The books will do it for me. He like my buddy and the majority of the world, is religious. They say they aren't but if you believe in a spirit, believe me you are. Religion created the spirit world disease, and contact was about to cure it. They all say they're not religious but have a relationship with "Jesus Christ." When I ask them where he is and what he is, they say he's in heaven and it's a spirit realm.

The Jehovah's Witnesses' evidence exemplified this reality. (See pictures.) The picture-taker and his denial that the saucer was real would write this ending. Johnny's lack of disclosure proves that contact will cure religion. This discovery will happen in 2004. I hoped the picture-taker would change. I predict he will. He does! But this won't happen until 2005, and he will still believe in spirits. Hell, this is my job to finally "reveal" and lead these aliens/angels to save the Earth. Man, this is unbelievable. But you will know his name then. Hang on, because we will go on tour. My buddy Jake and I severed our duo back in 2001. Wow! Could this be the reason the dream was set in Nashville in the first place?

It obviously is because it ends in Nashville. It still ends with two witnesses, me and Johnny. The world doesn't believe "just" me and Jake ain't ready like the picture-taker. But they all believe Johnny. Remember the scripture: "Many are last that shall be first and many are first that shall be last." Johnny is with me at the end. He's "hurt" by mankind's misery. He will embellish this pain in his award-winning Grammy song later this year. He's ready to be equal again. His video will make it painfully clear that "All is vanity."

We were about to pull in the restaurant when all of a sudden the radio played Johnny's new song. I got out of the car with tears in my eyes. I couldn't believe what was happening. Something was telling me to remember this. I couldn't wait to see the video. I knew it would be powerful. It was! I would cry again. I would soon find the picture. We had a great dinner and kept our conversation about the kids and school. We told them everything went great at the signing. They knew better; well, at least Jimmy did. Little Jake was too busy playing Game Boy to care. I was thankful for his lack of understanding. I cherished every moment. I knew it would be short-lived.

The dream flooded back. I was glad that he would be an adult when they returned. I felt like he would handle it better. I wondered how contact would go. I wondered all the time. I was going to write about it. I was going to tell the world how it goes! Man, what a job. I had to do some major studying involving quantum physics, relativity, and history. I also needed to put together a time-line that will clearly prove this separation. The fall is man! I would finally clear up where hell is! It should be pretty easy with the Mother-goddess statue's age. It was eight thousand years old. We had six thousand years of recorded history. I thought about the tenth planet's orbit. It took seven thousand years to make a full rotation, and it was on its way back. And according to the Bible we will have a thousand-year reign of peace upon their return. Six plus one make seven!

Duh! Is this planet used as a giant spaceship or another Earth prison? Would it really take a thousand years to make this transition? I had a million questions. I knew contact was just the beginning of what was about to happen. I knew there would be people who would refuse our real existence. They will try and run but they can't. So they will fight us. That's the obvious torturous truth about us. (See Cernes Giant.) They will have to be exiled again to another Earth. (See Hopi prophecy.) And not because we make them; they want to be humans. They don't like ugliness and equality. I can only hope that my children and the children of the world see man for what we are. "All is vanity!"

The next few months flew by. I couldn't stop my deja vu. It was happening all the time now. It was even happening to my son Jake. He was more aware of it since I was writing about it. He just had his twelfth birthday. Wow! No wonder it's the age of understanding. It implicates the twelve signs of the Zodiac and ten planets. Of course, you have to add the sun and moon. We do have to have them to live. We do have twelve months and the Jews have the twelve tribes of Israel. Greeks have twelve Gods!

I thought about the number seven and the number three. They are universally woven into all religious stories. According to the Sumerians the Earth is the seventh from the tenth counting in and the third from the sun counting out. The language of the ancients had an uncanny correlation to today's knowledge. How is this possible unless pre-destination really exists? We started with one language and will end with one. I was shocked to read about the Egyptian gods. They were just like the Greeks, a pantheon. But they only had nine like our nine planets. "Atum" made the nine gods. However, they were all considered one like the Jewish trinity, so it made ten! The amazing thing is that their creation story mimicked the Big Bang theory and my analogy of the Jewish story.

The Jewish star matches the atom, and its story begins from nothing. "In the beginning Heaven and Earth are void and without form." Wow, two things but one, like the yin and yang. Their god is spirit and omnipresent. They both have no beginning nor ending. This is the atom. Our modern science teaching of the Big Bang and religion's god have a contradictory teaching. They both have a beginning but don't have time and can't be created or destroyed. My whole point is that this is a contradiction. Atoms and heaven don't have a beginning or ending. It's all about image. Nothing ever stops existing; it just changes form. The trinity is the three stages of matter. Always changing from a gas to a solid to a liquid.

Back to my analogies of the past corroborating today's science. The first man of the Jewish bible is called Adam. The first Egyptian god was called Atum. Atum mixed with the great void called nun to create the other lesser gods. The name for Atum after this mixture was Ra-Atum. Come on! This sounds just like raw atom. It is what everything is made of, including us. Every creation story involves two elements. The Eskimos even tell of an egg with special fire inside. It fell from the sky and broke into two pieces. The visible stayed on Earth and the invisible fire went to heaven. Is this really a coincidence? The Yin and Yang really brings this point home. It, the AMA symbol, and the Jewish Star all reflect this principle of two things making one. They all have two parts, two pyramids, two snakes, TWO SPERMS in an EGG. The tribal people have a creation story that begins with a big egg having two parts, the visible and the invisible. Coincidence? The invisible/visible Polynesian god's name is Make-Make. He made all the others, and they are all equal even though they are lesser. The Paiute Indians god is hav-musums. This sound like must have! The infinite symbol is a figure 8 like cell multiplication.

I realized the story of Adam and Eve involves two elements themselves. The trees in the Garden of Eden number two. We have two chromosomes, x and y. I would soon read a novel entitled *Chromosome Six*. It was written by a doctor working on conquering creation and immortality. Could it hold the keys to what we so desperately want? Could they give us immortal, youthful beauty? I wondered about this a lot because of Travis Walton's abduction and the ongoing abduction phenomenon. It seems obvious that beautiful humans are the ultimate commodity. Who can't relate to the joy of being worshipped/adored because of it? This makes our own creation story sound more logical with the worship element. Isn't it the premise of religion that god wants to be worshipped? This is why I am asking the world to look again at Yeshua's teaching that man is evil/flawed.

He is a servant. Yeshua detested the teachings of Moses and revenge. He said that we're all equal! God isn't greater than us, and he gave this scripture to prove it. "A father isn't greater than his son"! Then he said that the father, son, and Holy Spirit are one. He even said we are gods! Come on! Do we really need to question the ending and beginning of ourselves and the universe when we see circles filling the sky? Circles fill the Atom and they make us, Adams! Do we question where the wind came from? I don't think so—here, there, every-where!

But at every signing my readers want to know where the universe came from. Why? Is it because we want to make sure there will be ramifications for our wrong-doings? Is this our problem? Are we so obviously evil that we inherently always want to challenge payback? I think so. I have found this to be an overwhelming common denominator with us. It's obviously the reason we have a conscience. Deja vu, makes it clear that we are in a place that we shouldn't be. It is the reason we are afraid of it and the unknown/darkness. Because there we might find the "truth," and what if we aren't ready for it? This is my greatest concern for all of us, including myself. There is infinite misery with the gamble of life. Control it, and we can have it all. Well, except for curing mankind. But we can escape our own hell through science and help others. We must do mystery to ultimately serve the greater good of the universe and every living thing in it. Service is the greatest reward because you're in control. You're doing the sure thing according to Yeshua and Issac Newton. We'll "reap what we sow" because for every action there is an opposite and equal reaction.

Isn't that what winning is really all about, the glory of sharing our abilities with others just so we can tell them they can do it, too? We want perfection! And to get it we have to do it. My evidence will "hopefully" reveal two infinite creations, one by nature and the other by us. (See Yin & Yang.) The universe, which is made of atoms, gave us our alien body that could create and it created us. We are it! They are both infinite in existence but will always remain separate. We are a flawed creation due to our sexual weakness. (See Cernes Giant.) We are part animal, only much worse because we can temporarily destroy ourselves and the ecological world that gives us life. Therefore we are predestined to be recycled until we get it. (See Hopi Prophecy.) We must solve our mystery through knowledge. This is the tragedy of religion. It says everything besides them is wrong! (See J.W. evidence.)

I continued to find more evidence as the summer passed. My alien book was slowly getting attention. I had to walk a fine line with my anti-patriotic stance. We were in war! The cold hard reality of this war is that it didn't cure the religious terrorism problem. It got worse. I wish President Bush would've tried forgiveness and love instead of revenge and hate. He hated these religious zealots but couldn't see his own. He even bragged about how many we killed. I cringed everytime he gave a State of the Union address. Does this man really profess to be a follower of Yeshua? Do we really think that Yeshua would kill someone for hurting him or anyone else? No, he would love them and forgive them. This is logical. Do we really think that we can make others give up their pursuit of WMD when we have them? Hell, most of the world has them.

I thought about China again. I hoped this wasn't the prediction of Revelations and the final war. It was the last prophesied war before the two witnesses. It said the army had two hundred million. This is their number. I couldn't believe it. I had to prepare myself for the worst anyway. It was happening now. People were dying everywhere as a result of the Iraq war and rampant religious zealots.

The year 2003 went out with the usual glitz

and glamour. Our armed forces ousted Saddam and it topped off the president's year, I'm sure. However, the elections of 2004 would soon begin. We discovered that the intelligence about WMD was bogus. Saddam wasn't the threat that the president made him out to be. I felt so sorry for all those parents who lost children on both sides. War doesn't make peace, and one day this logic will rule. We honor Yeshua and Martin Luther King Jr., don't we? Then shouldn't we follow their example? It is what the United Nations was created for. They impose economic sanctions. The United Nations had been very critical of this war. We went in without their help. The oneness thing didn't matter to our president, just revenge. Saddam defied his dad!

I know the president has good intentions, but where are they? Why doesn't he start his State of the Union speeches by telling people not to applaud? Yeshua would. He gloated in this ridiculous, never-ending applause. The whole setting mimicked the whiteness of revelation and the angels worshipping god. It sickened me! Can't the world see how our country is run by white wealthy politicians whose whole agenda is to be worshipped?

They act like rock stars. No, worse. At least Bono of U2 said, blank the system, UNLEARN!

Why isn't anybody wanting to limit individual wealth? I will! This is the answer and cure for Saddam Husseins. They're wealthy and yet want to help the people. I always said this was the reason Yeshua challenged the preachers to give away their money. This was the ultimate challenge, to see if we're "spiritual" or not. This is what made my book the most dangerous. I couldn't believe what happened in the first part of 2004. Two things shook my world to the core. It was the Michael Jackson scandal and, of course, the flying saucer photo on the cover of this book. I found a lot more evidence of flying saucers and alien statues in our ancient past but I will only mention one, well, two. I laughed. (See pictures.) I started my first book with the Roswell alien and reveal at the end a Roswell alien autopsy tape. It is still on shelves all over the world and hasn't been proven to be a fake. Although, anybody can say it has. However, I have found two pieces of ancient art to corroborate the existence of this six-fingered alien. I found a statue from Kiev (Yugoslavia) that is eight thousand years old, and one from the Aztec. Not to mention that man was created on the sixth day in the Bible.

Oh, by the way there is new evidence revealing General Ramey's memo. It was in his hand when they took the cover-up picture. The picture was analyzed and the memo reads, "3 dead crash victims and 1 live one." Coincidence? Anyway, there is a lot more evidence to support this alien flying saucer existence; just review the pictures. I can't believe that people aren't already thinking this way. It's not hard to imagine us doing these things a thousand years from now, so couldn't others have already done this? The scientific evidence and religious stories agree. So do the visionaries of our time, like Jules Verne and Albert Einstein.

We have successfully isolated the gene in worms to make them live twice as long. We have conquered the human genome system. The Bible starts with Genesis. Genes are the genesis, just the beginning of scientific infinite possibilities. We have to have faith in the scientific evidence of infinity and quit fighting for the finite present.

Now let's go back to my Earth-shaking discoveries. First, let's look at the Michael Jackson scandal. I wrote these books under the pen name Michael to implicate contact by Michael the arch-angel of the Jewish story and my case for the alien existence. However, I do have a last name in the books; it is Jackson. Ironically I did this because of our similarity with the Jehovah's Witnesses. We were both raised under this religion. I didn't realize that we also shared addiction to beauty of the flesh. Of course, mine is just with beautiful women. I see them like I do my artwork. Michael was charged with child molestation for the second time. I wrote about him in my second book. He is the epitomy of a narcissist. He loves wealth and yet says he loves the children of the world and is spiritual. He is no different from all the other hypocrites who say they are spiritual and are wealthy. He even has many paintings of himself followed by masses of children. It's as if he loves to be worshipped. I can understand how he got this way. He is a follower of a Jewish God that "demands" to be worshipped!

And then it happened he goes to trial and in the presence of an adoring crowd jumps on top of his car and does a dance for them. He does this while his private entourage is filming him. I don't know what will happen to him, and I won't predict it. But if he doesn't give up his money he isn't spiritual! And a child being molested isn't a funny "sideshow." Innocent or guilty it should be treated seriously!

The year 2004 continued. I was stressed out doing these signings. But I found more and more evidence of the flying saucer existence. There was even a general releasing photos of black objects in reconnaissance photos from Iraq. He was a Christian and was saying this was evidence of Satan at work. The president appointed him chief of the intelligence commission in Iraq.

They looked like flying saucers. I was blown away by the photos and the general's religious stance. I was especially blown away by his appointment. I followed this story. Man, I was always shocked at the sun looking like the atum and Jewish star when it was filmed. It shot out six perfect beams of light. We had a cave sculpture of this phenomenon. It showed the sun and the three planets on a grid. How is this possible? It was twenty thousand years old. I found even more evidence of the ancients knowing the structure of our solar system. A particular sculpture of rock art in Japan not only showed the exact structure of our solar system, but had ten planets and showed the third and fourth connected. This is Earth and Mars. (Look at satellite on Sumerian clay tablet of Mars and Earth.)

The Sumerian tablet proves this existence, and it shows flying saucers on the Earth side. The Mars side is holding the atom. It's obvious that contact is about nuclear war. The Cernes Giant has three knots on the club. The atom has three components. The Hopi prophecy shows the Earth with a line through it. The return is all about saving the Earth from us and nuclear war! That's the reason I use my first name only. It is also the point of contact in the Jewish story and why it is made.

"Michael will battle the kings of the Earth and save it from those who destroy it." I like the fact that I do it with the double-edged sword of my mouth. I talk! I found the hats of all cultures to mimic flying saucers. Hell, the Indians even used feathers, but the Chinese and Middle Eastern rice hats and turbans really looked like them. The bald heads of Monks do too! I found a book with ancient art of flying saucers and put a Chinese drawing from the nineteenth century in here along with another aborigine drawing. I did this because of Roswell and the saucer hieroglyphics on the space ship. These both contain this supporting evidence and the need for gold to make ozone layers. No wonder gold is important to planets and space exploration. It is where we live and they work. "Heaven/space is god's throne and the Earth is their footstool."

The aborigines used quartz to communicate with these gods. The Indians of Kentucky were mining it in Mammoth Cave. The Mayan skull is crystal. Crystal is a natural conductor of piezo electricity and stores memory! Quartz is universally revered. I read more about the head molding mystery. It was a universal practice by early man! They knew what the gods looked like. I was overwhelmed by my findings. I put a picture of Spontaneous Human Combustion. Their feet were left behind. Does this tell us something, like we might not need them? They must've conquered gravity because we have religion's levitation practice.

The Olmecs had a religious game that looked like a chess set. It had black players, white players, and one that was red. The giants of Easter Island mirrored this exactly, except on a larger scale. I interpret this as the struggle of creating humans, the red guy. Red represents creation and DNA. Look at the six strands of rocks below the largest Easter Island statue, the one showing the flying saucer on his head. It looks like a DNA print-out. This goes back to my point about the sixth chromosome and the Jewish creation on the sixth day. I found ancient statues of airplanes, astronauts, and rock art showing an alien observing an animal from a crane. THE OLDEST ONE IS FROM TASSILI AFRICA. It is fifty thousand years old!

I showed them to everybody and pressed on. I had given so much money away that I had become a magnet for anyone needing it. They all needed it! Well, most anyway. I'm afraid of absolute; I could be wrong. It is the first step toward humility, and we should always be humble. There! I only have one absolute. Anything is possible through humility! Well, I'm going out on a limb and say magic doesn't exist and man is evil. The aliens are the Gods of primitive man.

All right, it's time for the second earth-shattering discovery. Since I can't make these angels or aliens show and the story is "predestined" anyway, the next best thing is hard evidence by a universally famous person. I found a picture of Johnny Cash looking at a flying saucer! It was taken by another famous country music star. He said it was a hubcap. I would have gone to Johnny himself, but he died at the end of 2003. I know the picture-taker and he is famous; Johnny was, too. I can only speculate that they were and are protecting their religious traditions. Contact will eliminate it. I thought long and hard about this photograph. Everyone that saw it said it was a flying saucer. Well, almost everyone. I laughed. I think that most people were glad the picture-taker claimed it is a hubcap.

My insistence that we are "ugly" aliens seemed to torture everyone. Hell, who wants to be ugly? Well, remember with knowledge and practice anything's possible. Maybe, just maybe, even the best of both worlds. Anyway, I relentlessly pursued a picture that would match it. I found it! I couldn't believe it. I found a picture taken by Paul Villa in 1969. He was ridiculed and apparently met a tragic end. However, it is not in vain. The picture of Johnny Cash was taken twenty years later! They are a perfect match! It wouldn't matter if they didn't look at all the other evidence. (See pictures.) But they did! Everybody loves pictures.

I wrote this book and released it without the picture-taker's permission. I didn't do it for the money and I could've been wrong. But the "up" theme of religion clinched it. It wouldn't take long before he called me. He wanted to talk. When we met I immediately asked him if I could be Jesus. He believed in Jesus. He said that I wasn't. I reached and pulled out my wallet. I gave him my money and then started to wash his feet. He tried to stop me. I asked him to do the same for me. He wouldn't. I did it for him and when I finished he was crying. I hugged him and we both cried. I told him that I wasn't Jesus; that my name is Michael. He understood. I was the one who would "reveal" the angels and save the Earth from our impending global nuclear war. Reveal is the key word like "pretty" was to the angels in Genesis when they saw the daughters of man. I knew that he still rejected the ugliness of the aliens like my friend Jake. I told him that he will see Johnny at the end, and he would be an alien. You see, I told him Johnny sees this for what it is. All is vanity! It's even pre-destined which makes their "free-will" contradictory.

He cried tears of joy at the thought of seeing everyone again. I cried with him! I had already finished this book. I told him it was out! Well, he couldn't stop what had already happened, and he didn't want too. He was getting older like Johnny. He had lived the life of being adored and worshipped as a rock star. He was ready to give me my dream. I love music. We went on tour in 2005 and released the self-titled album, *M.D.* We called ourselves the country doctor. My name is the initials, Michael Duane! Our title cut was called "Just in Case." It was Jake's song! Our second release was Lester Flatt's wife Gladys's prescription to the world. We did a remake of "Rollin' in My Sweet Baby's Arms." It was a smash. The cover had M.D. in the center, the title cut below it, and the prescription at the bottom. At the top it read: "You better come see . . . the Doctor 'just in case.'" Then Gladys' prescription. We sold out everywhere we went. I was recognized as the producer of it all. However, I didn't want to be worshipped. I just wanted a chance to play music "for the love of it."

The Future Alien Contact

I wrote this song with George Jones and dedicated it to the unsung heroes who never had a cut. I manage to sell him some of my artwork while pitching my songs. He gave me the hook and told me that's why he does music. It ain't about the money, he said, it's for the love of it. I agree! I included Mrs. Lester Flatt in the song as well. She sacrificed her career to adopt Lester's sister's daughter. Lester's sister and husband died of a fatal disease within a year of each other. It was the very least that I could do for her. She was eighty-nine now and still performs with me. She'd done so much for all of us. After all, she is my wife's grandmother!

I didn't get to do music very long with Jake. He totally disagreed with my alien theory. He believed in spirit. However, he continued to do mystery. This is important! It is the way to transfer memory from one body to another. And yes, the future is all about creating beautiful humans, body parts, and power. It is what creates this ongoing mystery of mankind. This is all about power through our addiction to beauty of the flesh. We can return through bio-rhythm feedback. Time to up-load!

The future flew by. I was working on the unified field theory of quantum physics. I got a picture out of *Discover* magazine that showed our universe timeline. It did point out my theory that the word *beginning* was debatable. They finally questioned it. I couldn't believe it. They even alluded to the universe being a cyclical dance of creation. I laughed because that's my black hole/white hole theory of the yin and yang. The theory is based on the universe being membranes floating in nothingness. These "brains" for short are like flat flexible computer chips, and when they get close to each other they cause waves. I laughed at this wording, mem-"brane." It sounded like memory and brain. That's really all we are, information. The universe is black space like recording tape and we are the electrical device being recorded. Huh! This is macrocosm science. The universe looks just like us. (Check out picture of universe.) The picture looks like our cells and the DNA surrounded by mitochondria. It looks like e-stings! Well anyway, this in turn causes. . . !

Oh, enough of this; read *Scientific American*, *Discovery*, or any other science magazine. Anyway, this creation mimics the Yin and Yang white hole/ black hole thing. It is a never-ending cycle of reincarnation. That's the point of conquering space to stop it. We can conquer space and this dance with flying saucers. They looked like solar systems, galaxies, and the atom. I knew spinning fast enough could render something invisible. But could it free us from "flat" matter into space? Solar system, galaxies are flat. Read on! Space is the Egyptian Nun, nothing. And if we use our scientific mind we can preserve our mortal/immortal matter! Religion and science are both trying to conquer matter and be free in space. But religion creates close-minded, self-righteous anger. They don't accept new scientific discoveries. (See J.W. evidence.) That's the reason religion has to be banned. Religious war was everywhere!

Jake never pursued the alien evidence. We didn't do much together. I did cut some of his songs and he stayed active writing songs. He was brilliant at it! It's sad that his singing was never recognized by the world, but this is all vanity anyway. It was recognized by us.

The years flew by. The world escalated into

full-blown religious war. We invaded North Korea, and Communist China went on the offensive. We got too close. They proclaimed that our religious stance was nothing more than terrorism. We aren't the leader of the world. They ordered us to back out of North Korea. We didn't have a leg to stand on. We had WMD, so why couldn't others? We had the highest crime rate in the world, the highest suicide rate, the most aggressive history of conquest. Who says we're the best? All of a sudden our might makes right stance was being challenged by someone just as mighty.

I was petrified for the whole world. I knew it was just a matter of time before we dropped a bomb on North Korea. The Olympics started. It was December 1, 2012. I finally got world-wide attention. My books had become huge blockbuster movies. I always laughed to myself about our fascination with movies. It mirrored the gods watching us. I challenged the Jewish professor to come and talk about his mother-goddess. I was the keynote speaker for the opening ceremony. He refused. I challenged him if he didn't and the rest of the world to give up their money for the sake of science. I was interviewed several times before the show and expressed my desire to have religion banned, cap wealth, and chart a scientific course for the world.

I was about to go to the Olympics in New York City. I talked with Jake and he wasn't going to show. I told him it was okay. It was something I was supposed to do, not him. After all, the world selected me. I had helped the scientific community make huge strides with quantum physics and the completion of the unified field theory. Space travel wasn't about speed and distance. It was about the science of matter itself, the universe, and the unified field theory. That's why we see when we're out of our body. Our memory is traveling from one brain to another. Memory is the mem-"brane" of space. Everything is connected through atoms and energy!

I went alone. I didn't want anybody harmed in case my last dream came true. Hell, I've been shot once already, and it was a dream, wasn't it? The second book is happening now. This is its end. I wondered if I would get shot. Was I living this again through memory? It hadn't happened yet, had it? But I know I dreamed it. I was so confused and scared. Tomorrow was the day. Jake would be here according to my dream and I did get shot.

I was in the motel room. It was deja vu all over again. I called Angel and the kids first this time. I took a bath afterwards and then climbed onto the bed naked. I remembered back to the dream in 2003. I closed my eyes and sat back against the wall to do mystery. This is how my dream ended. Jake told me that I had to remember I had to do the mystery.

I woke up! "It time," he said bluntly. Jake was an alien and we were on the spaceship. I was an alien, too. I was the one in the driver's seat. It was my ship! No wonder they call us archangels! Jake wasn't ready to be the alien, I was. He was doing mystery. I needed to remember what happened tomorrow.

Listen to me. I'm talking like it has happened already. Somehow I knew it had! I got goose bumps and started to shake, sweat was running down my forehead. Wow! I couldn't believe what was happening. A tear rolled down my cheek. I smiled and closed my eyes. I was immediately surrounded by darkness. My heart was pounding wildly. I calmed myself and stopped my brain activity. I slipped deep into the mystery. It seemed like I lived in an eternity of peace before the Sun suddenly blinded me. It looked like the atom.

I was looking out over the crowd. I was there. I was at the Olympics and giving my speech! I was about to speak when a shot rang out. I felt the impact in my shoulder. It felt as if I had been hit by a sledgehammer and sent me crashing to the floor of the podium. The people started screaming, and complete panic broke out. The crowd went into mass hysteria. I remember trying to get up but they made me lay down. I was bleeding profusely. I tried to get them to let me talk. I needed to call Angel and the kids. I needed to tell them its all right. They assured me that they would call her, but told me to lie still. I tried again and then I saw Jake. What…! I blacked out.

The next thing I know I was in a hospital. Nurse Gail and Mom were at my side. She was stroking my hair.

"Where's Jake?" I asked quickly. I saw him at the Olympics. I tried to get up. Mom held me down but with great care. I knew this wasn't the end. We weren't in Jerusalem.

"He and Misty are with Angel and the kids,

Mike," Nurse Gail said quietly.

"What . . . are they all right?" I panicked and tried to get up again.

"Mike," Mom pleaded. "Please lie still; they're all right."

"Then why aren't they here? I need to see them." I looked at Mom and she looked at Nurse Gail. "What? Please tell me what is going on?"

I pulled Mom's face back to me and she was crying. "What is it Mom, please?"

She collapsed into my arms. She started shaking and crying convulsively. "Please don't," she begged.

"Please don't what, Mom?" I tried to lift her up and couldn't. She just hugged me tighter and tighter. She began to cry uncontrollably. Her body heaved as she sobbed again and again. Nurse Gail began to comfort her. I looked her in the eye. She gave me that look, and I calmed right down. Who is this woman?

"Do I know you?"

"Yes," she said so lovingly. "I was the first to tell you."

"Tell me what?"

"That you are Michael the archangel."

I couldn't believe it. I remembered her. I had given her husband a book. She came to me the next day and told me I was Michael the archangel. It really took me by surprise. She looked so much like an angel with her long flowing blonde hair and beautiful peach skin. She looked like my mother. She was breathtakingly beautiful. I never saw her again after we hugged and both cried. I never had anybody else say this to me since. She was the only one. No my mother finally did, too!

I broke into tears. She grabbed me and hugged me. She was crying, too. "You are him," she said as she began kissing my tears away. "Please don't cry."

I opened my eyes and looked deep into hers. "But these are tears of joy now. Please tell me why my mother is asking me not to go."

Nurse Gail lifted Mom up and hugged her. Then she gave her that same look that calmed me. It worked. They turned toward me and said they would show me what was going on. They turned on the television.

"Oh my god, no!" The world was on the

verge of global war. The picture lit up and showed explosion after explosion. We attacked Korea! Then it switched to the Middle East and showed reporters ouside the presidential palace. Terrorists had the reporter at gunpoint. Then it switched to the White House where another reporter was being held by gunpoint. Then it happened! They showed a reporter outside a hospital in New York. A terrorist was holding a gun to her head! Then it hit me. They wanted me. They wanted me to come to Jerusalem Israel!

"Oh my god, Mom, please tell me the kids are all right." I began struggling and trying to get up. I was panicking.

"Mike, Misty and the kids are fine; please calm down. Let me tell you what is going on."

I looked and saw the fear in her eyes. I knew what was going on. They wanted me. I had done it. I had pushed their buttons too far. The religious zealots saw this as the perfect opportunity for an ultimate Holy War. Our religious president had attacked North Korea and they were seizing the opportunity to do the same Religion versus Religion. They wanted me because I challenged the president and his magic religious god. Armageddon would be Science versus Religion and in their holy land! I was challenging god's existence and our religious president before attacking North Korea. The terrorists were calling us hypocrites, for killing and yet saying that a person who really knew god wouldn't kill. But they were doing it themsleves. The religious disease was everywhere!

We were the epitome of religious hypocrisy. The president wanted them to disarm their nuclear weapons and to stop making them, but we didn't. He was enforcing peace through war and his god was blessing it. It was crazy. Can't he see that a killing god causes all this insanity? Why can't they all see peace is the only answer and we can't have it with religion leading the charge? Why doesn't our president see that Moses' teaching are cruel and vengeful and the opposite of "turn the other cheek"? Can't he see that honoring the Old Testament is the same religion that these terrorists have. Moses and god is a killer! God kills his children! We are killers. Why can't everyone see this!

"Mike," she started to speak as her voiced quivered.

"I know, Mom, they want me to come to Jerusalem, just like I wrote in my book."

She nodded her head and started to talk again. I gently put my fingers over her mouth. "I know," I told her softly. "They want Jake, too."

"I knew it from the moment I saw him at the Olympics. He knew I was cured. I knew he wasn't. That's the reason he stayed away for so long. We knew our problem. I killed mine a long time ago. He knew when."

She started to cry, again. I reached and pulled her to me. I whispered into her ear and hugged her as tight as I could. "Go ahead and cry, Mom, the end is almost here. Our mystery and misery is just about to end, for us all. It's time to be happy and rejoice. Our future lies ahead and it is bright. We can't hide anymore from ourselves. Mankind is an evil scientific creation. The aliens are nature's creation. We're about to destroy this paradise and our prison. We need their help. Our planet needs their help. We must be stopped, now, before we destroy ourselves. Then I realized it's not about us, it's about planets. Earth's are nature's miracles. Infinite precious miracles." Nothing ever stops existing just because it ends. It's the law of nature, energy itself.

"Mom," I ended after hesitating. "We can't destroy ourselves, we must find ourselves. Existence is the ultimate miracle. We must desire to be an alien again."

She softly said, "I know that now." I looked deep into her eyes and could tell that she did. Then I looked at Nurse Gail. We all knew. I looked at the television and the terrorist was making his way toward my room. I told Mom and Nurse Gail to help me stand. I would go with them. They did and told me they were going too.

"I know, remember, I wrote about it."

The door swung open and the terrorist barged in. He was followed by a camera crew. The whole world was going to see this. He threw the nurse to the side and immediately grabbed me. I winced in pain and groaned out loud. My mother started toward me, but Nurse Gail caught her.

"They won't hurt him," and she looked toward the terrorist.

He didn't hurt me. He took me out of the room. I knew where we were going. We made it to the front door and I thought about Jake. I hoped he would turn himself in. A cell phone rang just as we were exiting the front entrance. Whose phone was it, I wondered? About that time one of the terrorists came over to us and reached the phone toward me.

"Here," he said sharply, "Talk to him and find out where he is."

I got on the phone and talked with Jake. He assured me the kids were all right and he was coming to the airport. I told the terrorist. It was all set. They wanted him, too. They wanted the "Two Witnesses"! We were headed to Jerusalem. Jake made it to the airport at the same time we did. They took us to the jet and we flew out of New York City with the entire international Olympic world watching in vain.

They had us strapped to a nuclear bomb. They wouldn't let us talk and the trip was grueling. I was in so much pain. Jake would hold me up and I knew that he finally believed me. He was the one who would be at my side. We landed in Jerusalem to a military escort, by everyone. Us, them, the Israelis, and the United Nations task force. It seems war was everywhere. And all because of this holy land.

Jihad is bullshit! The world's religious dis-ease. We were taken to their headquarters at one of Jerusalem's most posh hotels. We were put in a room until they made arrangements to state their demands. It seemed as if it were taking forever. Jake managed to tell me one time that I was the one to talk. "It was going to be quick," he said reassuring-ly. I knew it. But was I going to talk to the Israe-li who found the mother-goddess statue? Was that what this was about? Were they mad because I de-manded this scientist to debate my theories about god/gods and what they looked like? I was about to find out.

They took us down to the lobby entrance. We were on our way. The entire world was watch-ing. Cameras were everywhere. The scientist was on the stage. He was waiting for me. I was taken out first. The whole crowd starting throwing rocks at me. They still stoned people like the bible days. It really had the world brainwashed. The terrorists de-manded them to stop. They didn't. They even shot into the crowd. It was going to be a blood-bath. I looked back as they shoved me onto the stage and saw them bringing Jake. They pushed me in front of the microphone. The scientist stepped up and stood beside me. I nodded and he returned it.

He started by praising God. He said he believed that the mother-goddess statue had a head that symbolized fertility. He said it was a phallic symbol. Then he gestured that it was my turn. I chose my words carefully.

"This statue proves that the aliens are the gods of our ancient ancestors. Does a phallic symbol have eyes and ears? Please look at all the evidence. It is much older than our books. It shows us who scientifically manipulated primitive man. It shows us who their gods were."

A terrorist struck me from behind. He hollered that there is only one true god. I went down, but got back up. The scientist asked me where my gods were. I struggled to speak. I tried to tell them the aliens looking the same created theirs and religion's oneness. Suddenly, one of the terrorists came running out of the hotel. He started talking to the guy who hit me. He spoke English. North Korea launched a nuclear bomb against us. They also launched another one. It was aimed at Jerusalem.

"Please," I begged and turned toward them. They struck me again. I went down again. I heard him say that the United States had retaliated and struck many cities in North Korea. Then, I heard the worst possible news that I could hear. China was attacking the U.S.! They were doing this to save the world from this religious Jihad. They saw the U.S. as religious zealots!

I struggled to get to my feet. The scientist was wild eyed and screaming "Now, where are your gods?" I told them to forgive and love even those who hate you. I held up the peace sign. I knew there was nothing I could say. That's the cold hard truth about religiously brain-washed people. It would take contact.

He shoved me and demanded an answer. I looked at him and weakly said, "I believe in the aliens and they don't kill." He punched me and I fell backwards. Someone caught me just as I fell to the ground. It was Jake. All of a sudden, a shot rang out. I fell to the floor, but it wasn't me.

"Oh my god, they shot Jake." I turned and saw Jake. He was gasping for breath and had blood coming out his mouth. They shot him in the chest.

I lifted him in my arms. "I finally get it," he said and smiled. "Damn your killing god!" I screamed. He went limp in my arms.

"No," I screamed. "See what your killing god has done." I tried to stand. BANG, BANG, BANG! My body jerked violently and I fell dead. I came up out of my body. I went through the tunnel and back into my alien body. I was looking at Yeshua and two aliens, one on either side. I knew the drill. This was home! I was an alien. I wasn't finished. I had to do mystery. But first these events with Yeshua, then Jake, played out again. I knew what I had to do! I closed my eyes. The next thing I knew Mom was stroking my hair. I opened my eyes and saw that I was in Jerusalem. It was exactly as I had written it. I did get killed. Jake did too. And also an innocent young Jewish girl with a suicide backpack. How sad this disease is. Jake and I were the Two Witnesses! I was lying on a gurney and Jake was sitting in the corner. Sitting! And then it happened. I got up and told the world the aliens would take over and we all should do nothing to stop it.

Bombs were still being launched and now it's time. We are them. Suddenly, the camera crew was pointing out the windows to the sky. Flying saucers appeared everywhere. The televisions began showing them all over the world. The bombs had been disarmed. My ship was above us. Jake and I were teleported up, right through the tent. I saw Jake's alien body, Yeshua and his alien body. The glorified body! I rejoiced and hollered peace. I knew where I was. I was in the driver's seat!

I wept tears of joy. Mom and Nurse Gail were hugging each other. We approached them and Jake became frightened. Yeshua and his human form took Jake and his glorified body into the ship. I started to follow, but Yeshua motioned me to stay. I stayed, motionless, suspended in midair. We were about twenty feet in the air. I turned back to the cameras and began to speak.

"I will return to Nashville and comfort my family. We will disarm the world and begin to recycle most of you to another planet," I said. Then it would be my turn to be Yeshua. We all must be him to be with him.

"Many are first that shall be the last and many are last that shall be first." This is a quote by Yeshua on the second book. There were six billion who came and there are six billion now. Your science confirms this. I discovered this only last year, but already suspected it, with the universal teaching of reincarnation. We never stop exiting. It's all about science and change. Will you be willing to change? Will you want peace and oneness? This is scientific perfection. I warn you, "it is boring!" Now, we need gold for ozone layers and to continue life in space.

"Heaven's streets are paved with gold, they're planets!" I told them the other quote that was used on my first book: "If your days had not been shortened, no flesh would be saved." But now you know it always exists and mankind is cruel.

"This is why gold is so important and our symbol. You will soon know the wonderful truth about ourselves and the science behind it. You will only know if you seek it."

I touched the ship and said, "This is what I seek." The ship disappeared, but showed my alien body sitting at the control. Jake was beside his body this time, doing the mystery. "This is the way to find yourself." I brought Mom and Nurse Gail onto the ship and we headed to Nashville. We left in a flash and landed with Johnny and June Cash. But they weren't alone. In fact, they were themselves Aliens! I revealed ourselves and began to save the planet.

The picture of Johnny and the flying saucer is real and we are real. Man is the illusion, the flawed scientific creation. Don't be deceived. There isn't a cure, only separation. Time will tell, has told us before, and is telling us now. There isn't any time left for war. Science must prevail! We must save the Earth! The time is now, our struggle continues. The universe is a living wireless communication system and we/mankind are the virus. Spirit is the atom. It is the invisible hand that creates everything through movement. It doesn't think. Love of others is what should move us and that is the most important thing of all.

Don't be afraid of ruining your image. Beauty is only skin deep, to the near-sighted. There are far more important things to think about, like children. The less we think about ourselves and the more we think about the universe the better off we'll be. The better off they would be. This must be our treasure. Please consider that we "all" must be Yeshua sooner or later. We are one! I am Yeshua? Now, please give up your gold or find yourself being a gold-dig-ger again. Oh, by the way, digging is hard work! Re-member, don't be fooled by those who are rich and say they are spiritual. Our mystery starts here and ends here. It's all about the gold! Life is an infinite work in progress! I will see you soon! That time is now. Please look for my next book: *Crying My Heart Out Over You: the Mrs. Lester Flatt Story.*

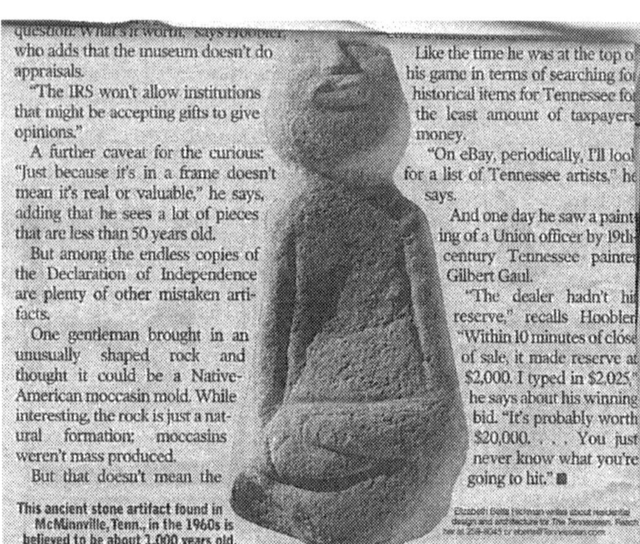

This ancient stone artifact found in McMinnville, Tenn., in the 1960s is believed to be about 1,000 years old.

This is how religion began and how it ends. The gods came from the sky and will return from the sky, heaven is space.

Earth's are footstools. They need our gold and we need them to save the earth from us. Gold can repair our ozone layer (Hence god symbol of gold halo) and is essential for space exploration. We are them and are addicted to the unnatural SCIENTIFIC creation of modern man. Outward difference of appearances create power through beauty of the flesh. We are ALL addicted to outward beauty. This is all about power and gold. Follow the evidence. It doesn't lie. Man does. Mankind is our ad-DIC-tion! And we kill for it. (SEE CERNES GIANT) This statue is from Mcminnville, Tn., and is circa 1000 years old. (Notice a big round head like the aliens.) It is what it is, an indian meditating and looking up to his gods. He knew they came from the sky and that mankind is evil. This is why worshipping them was all about giving up his own existence. Todays religion's have made heaven a spirit realm or another dimension and man good. If you believe this way, then you better re-examine the evidence. If you refuse to do so or still believe this way, after doing so, then you could be religiously brainwashed. In my research, I have found that very few religious people search for physical evidence of what the god/god or angels look like. (Seeking the kingdom of Heaven) They just follow modern religion's interpretation of the same. They call this faith. Faith is the abscence of evidence. (Testimony of things unseen). In a court of law their case is groundless. The alien evidence is HARD SCIENTIFIC EVIDENCE RECOGNIZABLE BY A COURT OF LAW AND IS WITHOUT MOTIVE. Crimes are committed with motive. Religion is all about POWER/GROWTH! Man is our crime, religion is his scapegoat. I challenge all religion to produce EVIDENCE of a magic spirit angel/god or gods and their spirit realm. This is important because religion creates killers. The Jewish Bible dominates the majority of earth's population and it's god is a killer. This is a scientific scary fact. What if the aliens are the gods of primitive man, WWYD?

www.tennessean.com   THE TENNESSEAN   Tuesday, April 6, 2004   **7A**

Psychiatric testimony key to different verdicts for mothers, experts say

By LISA FALKENBERG
Associated Press

TYLER, Texas — Andrea Yates and Deanna Laney were both loving mothers who home-schooled their children and gave them names from the Bible.

YATES

Both also suffered from severe mental illness that ultimately led them to kill their children.

The verdicts they faced, however, could not be more different.

Yates is serving a life sentence for murder for drowning her five children in the bathtub in 2001.

LANEY

Laney, who smashed her sons' skulls with rocks last May, killing two of them, was acquitted last week by reason of insanity.

Experts in Texas law, psychology and jury behavior say the opposite verdicts are largely because of strikingly different psychiatric testimony in the cases.

Psychiatrists in Yates' case disagreed on her sanity. But all five mental health experts consulted in Laney's case, including two for the prosecution, two for the defense and one for the judge, agreed she was insane, or unable to tell right from wrong. "It's a lot easier for the jury in a case like to that to find someone guilty by reason of insanity because they can rationalize 'Who are we to question the uniform conclusions of all the experts here?' " said Brian Serr, a law professor at Baylor University.

"In the Yates case, when you've got the experts disagreeing, now you're leaving it up to the jury to decide which experts to agree with."

Another potentially significant difference is that the jury in Laney's case learned that she believed God told her to kill the children; however, Yates said she was prompted by Satan.

Dr. Park Dietz, the psychiatrist who testified at Yates' trial that she knew her actions were wrong and therefore wasn't insane under state law, testified last week that Laney was a textbook case of insanity.

He concluded that psychotic delusions made Laney incapable of knowing right from wrong during the killings, the legal standard in Texas for insanity.

Experts said the nature of the crimes may have also swayed jurors.

As brutal as both cases were, it may have been easier for jurors to stomach beating children to death than drowning them, they said. ■

How sad for these children, that the last moments of life was spent looking into the eyes of a vicious killer and it is their mother. Worse, they don't understand how this can happen and don't die immediately. They struggled, pleading mercifully with their mother, not to kill them. She refused and they struggled again and again. What a nightmare! Imagine for yourself, what it must have been like to see your mother coming at you, to kill you! She's not supposed to do this. She is supposed to be the most sacred and safe haven in this scary world of uncertainty, death, and hell. But, somehow at this moment she isn't and you are so afraid. "Why are you doing this, mommy?" you plead. She grabs you and begans explaining that she's killing you for "love". You start crying in utter disbelief, fear, and desperation. You beg and beg only to see a blank expression. She isn't crying. In fact, she tells you to lay still and that she's doing this for "love". You gasp in horror! You realize this isn't your mother. She's sick. You fight back, you want to live. You are little and she is big, power prevails. It has always prevailed. Might makes right in the world of mankind. Then it happens, she kills you! This makes me shudder with horror. Worse yet, one "mother" gets life in prison, because she said the devil made her do it. The other gets off, for being found innocent, through the plea of temporary insanity. She said god made her do it! If this doesn't make you challenge the sick disease of religion, then nothing will. Apparently, not even the following scientific facts, about their sick "loving god/father". Their religious god could have it any way he wants, even perfect, if "he" chose too. Instead "he" made it this way. "He" made "our" world of hell, because "his followers", (who tell their kids not to be followers because of the obvious dangers) don't see the sickness of someone wanting/demanding to be worshipped or "we" will be killed. "He" created us to worship "him" and religion says it out of "love". These "mothers" said the same thing. Worship really means work for him! Follow the evidence to the gold. "He's" all about the gold, but supposed to bless the poor and hate wealth. Their "god" even chooses a favorite amongst "his" children.(another thing any "rational parent" would preach against) "He" orders Abraham, the top Jewish priest to kill "his" son Issac and many others including Moses to kill the egyptian slave. "His" killing is rampant throughout their bible. "He" ultimately kills the egyptians "himself", by closing the red sea back over them, when "he" could have let them go. Or "god forbid" make them perfect. Now, maybe we know where "god" forbidding the world to be perfect, comes from. Finally, "god" even kills "his" own son (I thought, that we are all "his" children) to prove "he" exists. Not to mention Sodom & Gomorrah, because he hates homosexuals. Last but certainly not least, "he" chooses to be a dead-beat dad, likes torture, revenge and hell, and kills "his" children as an example of "his" love to prove "his" power and to "make" us worship "him". What an example, for a "loving" father to set for "his" children, huh? Would we want this kind of a parent? I don't! How sick can this or anyone following this "guy" get? Well, these mothers killed their children, that's how sick. I'm sure they didn't want their mother to kill them. Then what made them this way? Well, you just read the facts, the evidence! Their god is a cold blooded killer and it is a scientific fact. Are they worse than God? They are the same. Look what this religion has done to its followers. If you are a follower you and your children could turn out this way. How will you react to this possibility. You can't say it wouldn't happen, because it did and still does. What would you say to your child, if he said god told him to kill your grand-child. If you tell them, that god doesn't talk to people, wouldn't you be a liar if you lived your life saying god talks to you and you talked to him? And if you faced this scenario, would you compromise by explaining, that god wouldn't tell anyone to kill their children or do it himself. If you do, then you are sick, like these women and are a brain-washed follower of a sick god "himself". This isn't the first time "his" followers said that god or the devil talked to them and told them to kill. Watch the evening news tonight, Israel will be on it! It obviously happened the minute religion began, their Cain killing Abel story! Oh and one more thing, I'm here to tell you, that the little voice in my head tells me everything under the sun. But, I am that voice and the love of children and all living things is my only reason to exist. I saw this woman, who was pitied and got acquitted because god told her to do this, show an emotional sign of relief at the verdict. It insulted my intelligence, just like "their magic loving religious god". It is only logical, as a result of these facts to conclude, that religion is "our" disease and killing for peace or love is illogical to any loving intelligent parent! I don't want revenge. I believe in the laws of nature. "For every action there is an equal an opposite reaction". I cried! I was tired of their God and Devil. He was a vicious old Southern white Christian. He'd kill me for God and say I was the Devil. It's all so twisted!

LOVE ALWAYS MICHAEL

One last thought from the author

The World Wide Web has made information universal and it mirrors the universal question of time itself. Does it really exist? Is it just a coincidence that these intials, WWW, also represent the three questions that plague mankind? What do extra-terrestials/angels/god/gods look like? (It's arrogant/self-righteous and un-provable to say we're the only ones.) Where are they? (The evidence supports their existence.) When are they coming back? (They don't have time and Einstein says it is relative.) The question of why they stay away is self-explanatory. (See Cernes Giant.) Do we really think this has only happened "once" in an "infinite" universe? Think about it! Remember the first law of physics. Every action creates an opposite and equal reaction. Maybe this "one" thing keeps happening over and over again!

Until we see otherwise, I'll take the safe bet. Scientific facts! My older brother Brian says to never "assume" anything. It makes an "ass" out of "u" and "me". Funny, as much as I crave knowedge, I didn't know this quote. Just goes to show you how little I know. I'm a college grad and he's a high school drop out. But he's a better man than I could ever be, because he assumes nothing. As a child, I lied on several occasions and caused him to get bad whippings from my dad and for this I'm terribly sorry.

Thanks, Brian, I love you and respect your wisdom. After all, you are my "older" brother. Funny, huh, even our fear of age implicates our addiction to beauty of the flesh. Challenge everything and follow no-one, especially not me. I am not worthy! I am ad-DIC-ted to outward beauty.

Let's face it: We all want to grow old . . . Just not look it!

Mike

P.S. Thanks Moze for your beautiful artwork! Special acknowledgments to Misty and Heaven, and to the love between this father and son, John and Gavin.

Contact me and find out more at my website, www.fortunecity.com/westwood/cerruti/1072

MICHAEL

MICHAEL

www.ingramcontent.com/pod-product-compliance
Lightning Source LLC
Chambersburg PA
CBHW022214050726
47590CB00002B/796